Birds, Bees and Butterflies

Iain Grahame

Birds, Bees and Butterflies

Daws Hall, a very special nature reserve and garden

Iain Grahame

with a Foreword by
Alan Titchmarsh MBE

Unicorn Press

For Bunny, with love

First published in 2019 by
Unicorn Press
60 Bracondale
Norwich NR1 2BE

www.unicornpublishing.org

ISBN 978 1 916495 76 0

Designed by Nick Newton Design

Printed in Belgium by Graphius

PHOTOGRAPHY
Most of the photographs illustrating the text have been taken by Katrina Grahame and the gardens photographer Nicola Stocken. Others are mainly by Bunny Grahame, Amy Sutcliffe or as listed below: p.34 Wikimedia Commons/High Contrast, p.115 Wikimedia Commons/Root AI & ER

Also by Iain Grahame: *Jambo Effendi*, 1966; *Blood Pheasant*, 1971; *Flying Feathers*, 1977; *Ruffled Feathers*, 1978; *Amin & Uganda*, 1980

FRONT COVER Giant Himalayan lily *Cardiocrinum giganteum*
BACK COVER Summer at the island pond
FRONTISPIECE 400-year-old cedar of Lebanon with ox-eye daisies

Contents

Acknowledgements

'Oh, God! The Major's bought another bloody tree' is a cry that, not infrequently, reverberates round this garden. The culprit, if I can call him such, is Jonathan Clarke who has worked here for over thirty years. His dedication and loyalty have been invaluable (and furthermore he takes as much pride in our small nature reserve and arboretum as I do). He has been helped by Melvyn Prentice, who has looked after this garden competently for a mere twenty-five years. A number of other kind people have turned their hands to a variety of tasks, notably Peter Johnson. A big thank you to all of them.

Particular thanks go to Simon Perry, our head teacher for close on thirty years. His inspirational teaching and broad knowledge of the natural world will long be remembered by the thousands of children who have had the good fortune to be taught by him. He was ably assisted, in turn, by Matt Carroll, Richard Wren, Sarah White and Holly Hilder; and now we have Amy Sutcliffe, a worthy successor to Simon.

I am immensely grateful to all past and current trustees, whose help and encouragement have been of huge assistance. Like all charities, we are permanently in need of financial support, and my hope is that this hidden gem, which gets no direct support from either Essex or Suffolk County Councils, will continue to be able to offer environmental education to children of all ages for many years to come. To all those who have helped and are currently helping, my heartfelt thanks. I hope too that this garden, which I have had huge pleasure in creating, will give pleasure and inspiration long into the future. Finally, I am very grateful to all those whose excellent photographs enliven the text, particularly those by my daughter Katrina and the gardens photographer, Nicola Stocken.

Iain Grahame

Daws Hall, 2019.

Foreword by Alan Titchmarsh MBE

Many people dream of owning a nature reserve; few of us can make it happen. But Iain Grahame has done just that and this is the remarkable story of the patch of paradise he and his family have created in the English countryside. From early days in Africa to the later years on the Suffolk/Essex border, Iain relates a charming story which is packed with surprises, from encounters with Idi Amin when he was nothing more than a private soldier, to beekeeping and the encouragement of butterflies and all kinds of wildlife in the carefully crafted landscape that surrounds Daws Hall.

There are glimpses into a lost world in these pages, but through it all shines the passion of a man and his wife who are intent on leaving their patch of British soil in far better heart than it was when they took it on. That, to me, speaks volumes, as does Iain and Bunny's determination that children who visit Daws Hall should be fired with enthusiasm for the natural world and encouraged to cherish it and play their own vital role in its future.

Conserving nature should not be an onerous chore. It requires energy and tenacity, certainly, but the rewards are many – not least the conservation and the well-being of birds, beasts and – most important of all – the insects, for without these often barely visible creatures we are all lost.

In our frantic and fast moving world, much is made of the bigger picture - nightly news bulletins bring ever more frightening stories of species being lost and land being laid to waste. So often we feel powerless to make a difference. The secret, I think, is to take action locally, on a manageable scale where the task is not nearly so daunting and where much can be achieved through will-power and determination, an understanding of how nature works and a well-formulated plan to improve the surrounding terrain. Iain and his family have done just that and my admiration for what they have achieved with the nature reserve and garden at Daws Hall knows no bounds.

Visit this entrancing place yourself and marvel at its beauty, at the diversity of species that you will see as you walk round, and at the commitment and achievements of the people who have made it happen. Where they have led, the rest of us should follow, for this really is a way we can make a positive difference to the future of our landscape and our wildlife.

The author, 1959

Stampede to Independence

In the early 1960s the Wind of Change was blowing across East Africa. Tanganyika was scheduled to gain independence in 1961, under the new name of Tanzania; Uganda was to follow in 1962 and then, finally, Kenya in 1963.

None of the many Britons that I knew during my time in East Africa resented these countries being granted independence; it was just a matter of timing. But many of us believed that it was simply too soon.

We were, however, a dwindling minority. The advent of increasingly left-wing teaching in the schools and universities of Britain and America, coupled with the understandable enthusiasm of Africans themselves to speed the process of self-determination, hastened what was already becoming a stampede.

With the benefit of hindsight we should have been better prepared. In Uganda, where I had served with a short break between 1953 and 1960, we had had a policy of recruiting almost exclusively from the warrior tribes in the north and north-west of the country. These Acholi, Langi, Lugbara, Kakwa and Aluru made splendid soldiers within the context of that time, and the presumption was that this situation would continue for many years to come.

There were, however, two big problems. First and foremost we were inadvertently encouraging tribalism. One has only to look at the bloody, internecine struggles between

4th Bn. King's African Rifles shooting team. The author, with Idi Amin holding cup

Kikuyu and Lwo, Shona and Ndabele, or Hutu and Tutsi, to see how little politicians of all political persuasions in Britain and elsewhere understood the strength of these age-old tribal loyalties and animosities, which were sadly still prevalent in Uganda. Secondly, there was the abysmally low standard of education in the army.

Idi Amin was a reasonably good platoon commander in my company in 1961. He was strong, smart, an excellent athlete, a first class shot, and the heavyweight boxing champion of Uganda. He was, however, virtually illiterate. The commanding officer had recently decreed that he and other senior Africans should be instructed on how to open bank accounts. Accordingly, I drove him down to Jinja, where the bank manager patiently explained about cheque books, bank statements and so on, and then the time came for him to give a specimen signature. The manager duly produced the relevant form, plus a pen, to which Idi responded with a blank expression and a big black thumb. (Thumbprints at that time were the accepted form of receipt for all pay, weapons and so on in the army). The manager, somewhat mystified, checked with head office and was firmly told that thumbprints were not an accepted form of signature. With some difficulty and after several laborious attempts, Idi managed to produce an acceptable scrawl of a signature. Little did any of us know that eight years later he would be President of Uganda.

The build-up to *Uhuru* in fact went remarkably smoothly, and incidences of drunkenness among our *askari* were no worse than usual. It was, however, a somewhat unreal time, with many of these *askari*, including Idi, saying 'please don't leave us, *Effendi*, we want you to stay and help us for many years to come'. As the big day approached, we went into overdrive with education classes and endless rehearsals on the parade ground. When midnight struck on 8 October 1962 Uganda became a fully independent and self-governing country. The omens were hardly promising.

Amin presenting me with a Lugbara *nanga* (part stringed instrument, part drum), 1975

Astride a white rhino, Rumuruti, 1961

My final three years in Uganda were in fact particularly enjoyable. When I married d'Esterre in 1960 we were given a nice bungalow just outside the barracks and we seized every opportunity to go off on *safari*. Nowadays that word implies looking at big game and other denizens of game parks or reserves, but the Swahili word '*safari*' literally means any journey or expedition, and this is exactly what we did. At that time the country was not only teeming with game, but the bird, butterfly and plant life was equally spectacular. I well remember going with d'Esterre to the foothills of the extinct Virunga volcanoes in the hope of seeing the elusive mountain gorillas. All day long our guide, Reuben, led us as we climbed through an almost impenetrable jungle of bamboo, following one small family group. We found their rudimentary 'beds', surprisingly high off the ground, which they had constructed and used the previous evening, and then we could hear them calling as they moved just ahead of us through the undergrowth. Finally we had the briefest of glimpses of a group of about six, led by a colossal male. On other occasions we went either to the Murchison Falls in the north of Uganda, where the river Nile tumbles through a gap barely eight metres wide, or to the Queen Elizabeth National Park close to the Congo. In the National Park it was then not uncommon to see elephants with tusks each weighing a hundred pounds or more. The game in both parks was so numerous then that it was impossible to imagine a time when many of the grasslands might disappear, the forests vanish, or that mankind could be so insensitive and brutal as to bring some of these magnificent creatures to the brink of extinction. At that time we were fortunate in having a commanding officer who not only allowed, but actually encouraged young officers to go off for long weekends with a military Land-rover and a couple of *askari* to 'wave the flag' in some of the remotest and least known parts of the country. d'Esterre and I never ceased to be amazed that ninety percent of the British officers and their wives much preferred spending their weekends around the swimming pool in Jinja, and only one couple, Hugh and Sheila, became regular com-panions on our expeditions and shared our love of exploring this wonderful country. Frequently, we would sleep out under the stars, knowing that a camp fire would always ensure we were safe from marauding lions or hyenas. Supper would usually consist of roasted guinea-fowl or francolin, shot by Hugh or me and cooked wrapped in mud, feathers-and-all, on the open fire. The Africans knew instinctively when the birds were ready to eat. After hoicking them out from the hot embers and giving them a sharp tap with a shovel, feathers and mud disappeared and what was left was definitely *haute cuisine*.

↖ *Papilio demodocus*

← *Graphium leonidas*

Butterflies and Bananas

Entomology, the study of insects including butterflies and moths, has been a lifelong interest. In England there is just one *papilio* or swallowtail, but in Africa there are around fifty different forms, most of which have wonderfully iridescent colours. It was not the swallowtails, however, that occupied my main interest, but another group of butterflies, the charaxes. At that time they were not fully known, due to the habit of the females of some of the species spending almost all their lives circling and feeding around the highest treetops. It was, needless to say, an exciting and challenging time to be actively involved in the collecting and classification of the all too little known African *charaxidinae*.

I remember on one occasion sitting in the shade of the Landrover, having a picnic lunch with Hugh, Sheila and d'Esterre. We had just spent a thoroughly frustrating morning in the Ituri forest, close to the Congo border, swiping with our nets with very little success at these elusive and fast-flying insects. We had had our excitements, however, notably watching giant blue turacos and a pair of black bee-eaters, but all we had to show for our efforts with our butterfly nets was one rather ragged specimen of a male of the commonest charaxes in that area.

It was Sheila who suddenly exclaimed 'look!'. We followed her gaze and, lo and behold, there were six or seven brightly-coloured charaxes feeding quietly on some object not more than twenty yards from where we were sitting. We crept up to watch and the butterflies never moved. It was then that I started to use my nostrils as well as my eyes.

'Leopard dung', I exclaimed triumphantly, and thereafter our success rate multiplied hugely. Leopards were then a common species in Uganda, so whenever we went off on *safari* we always made sure we had a liberal supply of their dung in the vehicle. Our catches increased, but the question remained – how to catch a female? Could it be that the Almighty, for some reason best known to Himself, had created a vast preponderance of male charaxes? It seemed unlikely, as this was not the case with any other species that I knew. There had to be an explanation and a way of catching them.

It came in fact several months later, when I was on a 'recruiting *safari*' in the northern province of Uganda. '*Simama*' (stop), I shouted to Okello, my long-suffering driver. (Africans loved to give Europeans nicknames and one of my nicknames was '*Bwana Kipeopeo*' or *Bwana* Butterfly). We had just been driving out of a native village and I had spotted, not only a pile of rotten fruit beside the road, but also what was clearly a number of butterflies on and around it.

Okello handed me my butterfly net – always carried in the vehicle together with the leopard dung – and within a few moments I had caught my first female *Charaxes bipunctatus*.

It was shortly after this that a good friend who lived in Nairobi told us of a Mr. 'Pinky' Jackson, who farmed near Kitale and was a recognized authority on butterflies, particularly charaxes. A quick telephone call resulted in d'Esterre and me being invited to stay with him the next weekend.

On our arrival he gave us a quick tour round his estate where the main crop was tea. He employed around a hundred African staff, but what impressed us most were the lengths to which he went to look after his men and their families. He had built a school and engaged teachers, for the vast number of children who rushed out to greet him, and also a dispensary with full-time nursing staff.

Back in the house, surrounded by bougainvillea of every conceivable colour, we quickly saw how he had got his name. d'Esterre and I settled for a cup of his home-grown tea, while he poured himself the first of what seemed like an endless series of pink gins. Like many heavy drinkers that I have come across, the gin seemed to have absolutely no adverse effect on him whatever. The conversation soon turned to butter-flies. He listened politely to the accounts of our rudimentary efforts to catch some of our local charaxes, and then went on to explain the stage to which he and a colleague, Dr. V. G. L. van Someren (an internationally recognized ornithologist and entomol-ogist), had reached. Interestingly, they had both progressed through the same stages as we had with leopard dung and rotting fruit, but were now using traps and cheap African labour. The collectors were given short courses of instruction before being equipped with a supply of light-weight mosquito netting traps, tins for keeping fer-mented banana, and cigar boxes for the storage of specimens. Many charaxes species are found in or near tropical rain-forests, and the African collectors were able to live and travel, mainly on foot and very cheaply, to a lot of remote areas. One of Pinky's collectors, he told us, was currently working for him in the Cameroons. Both Pinky and V. G. L. themselves trapped when they had the time, but – most exciting of all to me – they had found and described several species of *charaxes* that were new to science.

Visits to V. G. L. were equally memorable. A South African by birth and a retired dentist by profession, he lived alone in an isolated part of Karen on the outskirts of Nairobi. 'Alone' is not a totally accurate description. Despite announcing beforehand one's impending visit, the first sighting on rounding a corner of his private woodland was of an old man, standing on his balcony beside a bearded vulture, with a shotgun pointing in the general direction of one's midriff. After that somewhat hostile reception he was totally charming and a walking encyclopaedia on all matters relating to birds or butterflies.

Charaxes grahamei ♂ and ♀

Needless to say these visits inspired me to redouble my efforts with the charaxes. d'Esterre and I paid numerous visits to the Mabira Forest which was less than an hour's drive from the barracks. After setting the traps, baited with fermented banana, we would spend a leisurely hour or two bird watching before retracing our steps and collecting any interesting charaxes from the traps *en route*. The Mabira, together with the Kakamega Forest (close to the border with Kenya) and the Sekoke Forest (near the Kenyan coast) were fairly small but nevertheless important relics of the rainforest which at one time stretched right across the African continent. I used to visit these areas whenever possible for the wealth of bird and butterfly life that they contained. There was one memorable occasion when, putting out my traps in the Mabira, I came face to face with a small party of the rare dwarf or forest buffalo. My last visit to this area was in 1970. Gone were the giant blue turacos, gone were all the forest species of butterfly, and gone were the bushbuck, the dikdik and the colobus monkeys. The whole area was covered with neat rows of Arabica coffee bushes.

Three years after our visit, and shortly after Kenya gained independence, Pinky Jackson was hacked to death by a drunken member of his staff. He had no heirs; the farm was broken up into small lots, and the school and the dispensary were vandalized and burnt to the ground. Shortly before his death he had given his collection of African butterflies to the British Museum, and there it remains as a lasting memorial to a farsighted and remarkable man.

Part of my last few years in East Africa was spent as *aide-de-camp* to the General Officer Commanding, or G.O.C. Based in Nairobi, one of his responsibilities was to visit the various troops under his command in Kenya, Uganda, Tanganyika and Mauritius. On top of this he was encouraged to pay courtesy calls on the governors or rulers of other neighbouring countries. Where he went the ADC went too.

During the time I was in Nairobi I often spent a happy hour or two in the botanical gardens. Apart from all the exotic trees and shrubs, it was an excellent place for bird-watching. And that was how I got to know Peter Greensmith, who was responsible not only for the botanical collection, but also for the colourful displays of plants that could be seen along the city streets and outside Torr's Hotel and the New Stanley.

One day I happened to mention to him that the following week I was going to accompany the general to Ethiopia where, with a number of delegates from other countries, we would be celebrating the twenty-fifth anniversary of the return of the emperor, Haile Selassie, after the Italian occupation.

'Gosh', he said, 'will you be going anywhere near the emperor's garden?'

'Yes', I replied. 'I know there's going to be a reception at the palace the day after we arrive. Why?'

'Well, that is one of the only known sites of a very rare banana tree that I would dearly love to add to my collection. I've already got almost thirty different ones growing in the gardens here'.

Peter then explained that there were about forty known species of the genus musa, English name banana or plantain, that could be seen everywhere in East Africa and in many other parts of the tropics. He told me how to identify this particular species, of which apparently only a very few examples were known, and explained how to take cuttings.

'That shouldn't be too much of a problem', I said gaily, and promised to bring the cuttings to him as soon as we got back to Nairobi.

The flight to Addis Ababa went without a hitch and the general and I, attired in our ceremonial uniforms, together with the Ethiopian liaison officer who was looking after us, duly arrived at the palace gates at the appointed hour. The sentry gave a smart salute and then Brigadier Mengistu Newaye,[1] the commander of the Imperial Bodyguard, stepped forward and introduced himself.

He explained that we were going to walk a short distance through the emperor's private garden, and he would then usher us into the palace where we would be meeting His Excellency Haile Selassie himself. We had only gone a short distance when I spotted it, growing quite close to the path. Its large leaves were very faintly tinged with pink and

---

1 He was hanged, drawn and quartered, one month after our visit, for leading an attempt to overthrow the Emperor.

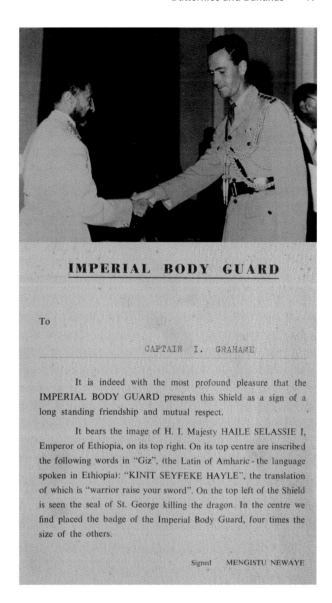

IMPERIAL BODY GUARD

To

CAPTAIN I. GRAHAME

It is indeed with the most profound pleasure that the IMPERIAL BODY GUARD presents this Shield as a sign of a long standing friendship and mutual respect.

It bears the image of H. I. Majesty HAILE SELASSIE I, Emperor of Ethiopia, on its top right. On its top centre are inscribed the following words in "Giz", (the Latin of Amharic - the language spoken in Ethiopia): "KINIT SEYFEKE HAYLE", the translation of which is "warrior raise your sword". On the top left of the Shield is seen the seal of St. George killing the dragon. In the centre we find placed the badge of the Imperial Body Guard, four times the size of the others.

Signed   MENGISTU NEWAYE

Meeting Emperor Haile Selassie. Below the photograph is the inscription on the small shield presented to me

were much more pointed than the normal banana trees that I knew so well. There was no doubt about it; it was just as Peter had described it.

I looked back to the sentry who was still standing by the gate, no more than fifty yards behind us. It should be a piece of cake, I said to myself. Come back by taxi with a torch after dark; tell the sentry that I was sure I knew where I had dropped my wallet earlier that day; give him a generous tip, and the whole job shouldn't take more than ten or fifteen minutes.

I was just firming up my plans for a little gentle kleptomania when we rounded a corner and there was the palace right in front of us. Nothing could have prepared me for the sight that then met my eyes. Chained to either side of the ornate entrance was an enormous black-maned lion.

Later that day I met up with Prince Alex Desta,[2] the emperor's favourite nephew, who I knew well from a visit he had made to Nairobi the previous month.

'Alex', I said, 'don't those poor lions ever get a chance to stretch their legs?'

'They're only chained up during the day' was his reply. 'They have the run of the garden from dusk to dawn, so we don't need to employ any night watchmen.'

And so ended my little plan for taking clandestine cuttings of rare banana trees. Shortly after this Ethiopian interlude, however, and to the rotting fruit of a different species of banana in one of my traps, ventured several charaxes butterflies. These turned out to be new to science, and V. G. L. very kindly gave them the scientific name of *Charaxes grahamei*.

In the autumn of 1963 my tour of secondment was over and I had already advised my parent regiment, the Royal Green Jackets, that I had decided to leave the army. And so, after an adventurous five years – part soldiering, part bird watching, part butterfly collecting, in the most beautiful country and with the most delightful people I know – we prepared for a new chapter in our lives. It was with considerable concern for the future of Uganda that I handed over my company to Idi Amin, and we returned to England.

Little did I know at the time that my involvement in East Africa was far from over. During the 1970s there were a number of occasions when I was asked by the British government to go back to Uganda on a variety of diplomatic assignments (see my book *Amin & Uganda*, 1980). I was also lucky enough to be invited by a well-known travel firm, during the 1980s, to run their up-market tented *safaris* in Kenya and Tanzania.

A few final words before we leave East Africa. Old people like me hardly dare now to mention colonialism, which to a lot of people is about the most contemptible word in the English language. The sad thing for us 'imperial villains', who lived and served in these once happy and prosperous countries, where elephants and rhino were fully protected, is that the descent into chaos, corruption and a reversion to tribalism was all too predictable. There is an Acholi proverb which goes '*Motmot ocero Muni poto*', which translated is 'slowness prevented the European from falling'. Or, 'slowly but surely'. If only …

---

2 He was *murdered together with the emperor and many of his family in the coup that took place in 1975.*

Back to my Childhood

Before moving on to the time when I went to Cirencester to learn about farming, I am going to wind the clock back a number of years, if only to explain a little bit about my childhood and how the natural world gradually became an all-absorbing passion in my life.

When war broke out in 1939, my sister Eila, aged four, and I, three and a half years older, were living with our mother, a nanny, and an Alsatian dog called Pup in a house called Poynters in Cobham, Surrey. I have no recollection of our father, a professional cavalry officer, ever living with us and it was only later that we were told that he had 'done a runner'. Along one side of the garden ran a stream, and it was there that I would spend much of my time exploring for frogs and newts and other strange creatures, some of which would end up in jam jars in our nursery. My other favourite place was a little meadow at the end of the garden which abounded with butterflies and day-flying moths. Armed with a net and cyanide 'killing jar' – all of this well before the advent of Health & Safety – I built up my first little collection, each specimen pierced through its thorax and then pinned into an exercise book. I also started a little collection of birds' eggs, but stuck firmly to the rule of only one egg per nest.

Childhood memories are often very dim, but I do remember, shortly after my eighth birthday, my mother sewing on name tapes, and Miss Newman, our nanny, giving me extra lessons in English and history which I loved, and maths which I hated. Then it was off to my first school, Ludgrove, where I soon experienced my first taste of discipline. Alan Barber, the headmaster, was notorious for caning his boys for what, in retrospect, were fairly small misdemeanours. However, we knew what to expect, we knew it was going to hurt, but we also knew in a strange, masochistic way that it was an early test of self-discipline and courage, qualities that we were all going to need in our lives ahead. I remember very clearly how proud I was when I nad notched up my hundredth stroke of the cane. That and winning the squash championship were my two triumphs at Ludgrove.

It was fairly soon after the start of the term, in 1940, that we all had a ringside seat at a 'dog fight' just over the school grounds, featuring a German plane and a British Spitfire. I remember the masters all shouting 'come outside and watch, boys.' We all downed our pens and pencils and rushed out of the classrooms, just in time to see the two planes manoeuvring in the air, each one trying to get into a position where it could release a lethal burst of ammunition into the enemy. In the end it all happened very quickly. There was a cloud of smoke surrounding the German plane and, just before it nosedived towards the ground, a parachute emerged from the smoke, and the German pilot floated down to earth. We all clapped and cheered. A police car appeared from nowhere and headed off to apprehend the German pilot who we later heard had survived unharmed.

What I also remember with startling clarity was Alan Barber taking me by the arm one sunny morning in early October, 1940, and walking with me to a stile beside one of the playing fields and telling me, in what seemed a fairly matter of fact way, that my mother had been killed by a German bomb. I've thought back to that moment on countless occasions over the years and I even made a point of revisiting that stile – still standing exactly where I remembered it – and realizing that I was just one of a number of children who had suffered a close family loss. Countless fathers, uncles, brothers (but probably not many other mothers) perished during World War II, and I was certainly not the only boy to whom ATB had to break dreadful news. What else do I remember about that morning? Two things: first, that I was excused all lessons for the rest of that day – whoopee! – and, secondly, I was very proud of the fact that I didn't blub ...

The early history of Ludgrove reads much like a story from a Boys Own magazine. Arthur Dunn, who founded the school in 1892, had two exceptional talents: he was a brilliant footballer and he had a superb singing voice. Two years after leaving Eton in 1880 he played for the OE's when they won the F.A. Cup Final against Blackburn Rovers in 1882. After Eton he went up to Trinity College, Cambridge, and then embarked on a teaching career at Elstree School. He enjoyed his time there, but one of the reasons why he left and founded his own school was that Elstree boys went to Harrow ... He was also an exceptionally good cricketer, with both bat and ball and, on one occasion when touring Ireland, took five wickets in five balls. (This was when there were only five

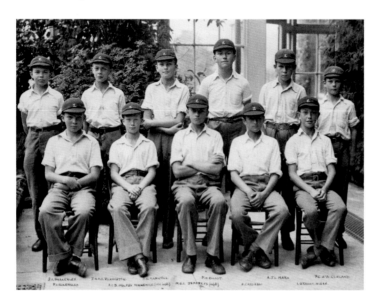

Ludgrove Cricket 1st XI. Front row: Colin Ingleby-Mackenzie 2nd from left, Iain Grahame far right.

balls in an over!) In the course of the 1900s he found time to play for the Eton Ramblers on a number of occasions, when he scored nineteen hundred runs and took ninety-six wickets for an average of eleven.

Not surprisingly, he soon persuaded a number of his friends, who were for the most part soccer internationals, to join him on the teaching staff at Ludgrove. These included two of the most famous players of the day, G. O. Smith and W. J. Oakley. During the early days of the school, when England was playing an international match, Ludgrove would almost cease to function. Dunn captained England at soccer for a number of years, and is remembered now by the Arthur Dunn Cup.

Alan Barber himself captained Yorkshire at cricket, and was passionate about encouraging his boys to excel at boxing, soccer, squash, fives, cricket and golf. One of my best friends there was Colin Ingleby-Mackenzie, the finest all-round sportsman of my time at Ludgrove and then again at Eton. I remember, when we were both aged about ten, challenging him to a round of golf on the nine-hole course there one day. Colin was left-handed and, when we went to where the clubs were kept, someone had already taken out the only left-handed set. 'No problem', he said and went on to par all the holes bar one, playing right-handed. At Eton he was captain of the eleven, captain of soccer, and keeper of racquets (where we both played for the school). After that he captained Hampshire at cricket, and scored a century against the ferocious bowling of Charlie Griffith and Wes Hall of the touring West Indies.

What else do I remember about that first term? There was the usual outbreak of measles (which I caught) and also of whooping cough (which I didn't catch). And then there were some older boys in my dormitory who used to take a delight in getting us new boys to run between the rows of beds while they flicked ties or belts at our bare backsides. Then there was soccer, skating on the school pond, and Mr. Barber having another chat with me. This time it was to tell me that, when the term finished, I was going to go to Suffolk, to a house called Loudham, where I would find my sister and where we were both going to live with our Uncle Denis (brother of my mother) and Aunt Madeline, who had a farm with lots of goats and chickens, horses and pigs. It all sounded very exciting.

The end of term came and off we all went by train to Waterloo Station in London. (Petrol was severely rationed in those days, so nobody undertook long journeys by car). There, on the platform, was Miss Newman – for some reason we never called her 'nanny' – and I remember going pink with embarrassment when, in front of my friends, she gave me a big hug and took my hand. Then it was crossing London by taxi to Liverpool Street Station, and everywhere we looked there were signs of the 'black-out' due to the Blitz. We got on to another train where we had lunch and, after about an hour and a half, arrived at Wickham Market station. Waiting on the platform was a grey-haired rather elderly lady, who I remembered I had met once before, who introduced herself as my Aunt Madeline. Like a lot of her contemporaries, she never drove, so Jack (part-time gardener, part-time chauffeur) took the wheel and after a fifteen minute drive through a light snowfall we arrived at what was to be my new home. A log fire was burning, a Christmas tree was standing in the hall, my Uncle Denis was reading the newspaper, and my little sister had her mouth full of strawberry jam.

After depositing me in the drawing room with the others, Miss Newman retired. As I began to settle in, I gradually began to get used to what seemed at first to be a rather strangely hierarchical pattern of life. My aunt and uncle had two children, both now married and with children of their own. The nursery wing, now long closed up, had had to be opened up for Eila and me. This was Miss Newman's territory and if she wanted anything she would ask one of the servants. With wartime economy these had been reduced to three – Buckley, the butler had just been caught helping himself to the contents of the cellar, so he was about to leave and was not replaced. Then there was Big Mary, the cook, Little Mary, her assistant and scullery maid, and various wives and daughters of the farm workers, who seemed to take it in turn to generally dust, sweep and clean in the house. Aunt Madeline had had a lady's maid for many years, but she had left shortly before our arrival. So, the house was really divided into three areas. The drawing room, dining room, 'smoking room' and the four or five main bedrooms belonged to my guardians. Then came the nursery wing with a further three or four bedrooms, where the two Mary's slept and, a little apart, we and Miss Newman lived, ate and slept. Finally, there was the kitchen area and the servants' hall, which was where Eila and I were frequently to be found. That was where the laughter, the gossiping and leg-pulling prevailed, and where we listened open-mouthed to the latest gossip, which invariably seemed to be of a sexual nature. I well remember one particular incident which was way above my small head, so, after a bit of discussion, it was Big Mary who was deputed to tell me about the facts of life. It all sounded pretty disgusting.

Looking back, what seemed perfectly normal in those days, but was so very different to modern day practices, was the fact that most of Eila's and my time indoors was spent in the nursery wing with Miss Newman. This only changed around four o'clock each afternoon, when Miss Newman made sure that our hair was brushed, our hands were clean, and then took us down to the drawing room where we had to be on our best behaviour. We spent about an hour there either listening to Aunt Madeline reading aloud to us, or playing card games. Beatrix Potter and Arthur Ransome were our favourite authors during our earliest days at Loudham, while Racing Demon was our best loved card game. Then it was a quick kiss and back to the nursery for high tea, piano practice, baths, prayers and bed.

Aunt Madeline was an Adeane, a family of five girls and, finally a son, Robert. The oldest girl, Pamela married George Lyttleton, the well-known Eton house-master, and they were the parents of Humphrey, the famous jazz trumpeter. Uncle George latterly came to fame through the publication of his correspondence with a former pupil, Rupert

Loudham Hall, Wickham Market

Hart-Davis, which lasted from 1955 until Lyttleton's death in 1962. Sybil was twice widowed, and she then married Roger Fulford, writer and prominent member of the Liberal party. Then there was Lettuce, who married Geoffrey Colman of mustard fame; and, finally, came Helena (or 'Twits') who married Willie Radnor.

Uncle Denis was always rather a remote figure in our lives. He had been badly gassed in the 'fourteen-'eighteen war and his health never fully recovered. Born in 1893 (the same year as Aunt Madeline) he had been an outstanding cricketer in his youth, being in the Eton eleven for no less than three years and captaining it in 1912. From there he went on to Oxford where, like so many of his contempories, his time was brought to an abrupt halt by the advent of hostilities. I never heard him talk about his time in the trenches, where he lost so many of his friends. His life when I knew him centred round the farm, shooting, his London club (White's) and cricket at Lords, where he would often join up with two famous cricketing friends, 'Plum' Warner and 'Gubby' Allen, both England captains in their day. During the Second World War he commanded the local (Woodbridge) Home Guard. I used to be fascinated, whenever I visited the gun room at Loudham, to find boxes of 12 bore cartridges each loaded with a solid lead ball. Fortunately, the Germans never invaded. His oldest and best friend was Mike Bowes-Lyon, a childhood and Eton contemporary who, with his wife Betty, was a regular guest at Loudham. I have at home my mother's scrap albums, in which there are a number of photographs of her, her two brothers, Roy and Denis, and sundry Bowes-Lyons, including Mike and his sister, who was later to become Queen Elizabeth.

I had only been at Loudham a few days when Uncle Denis rang the bell and sent for the gamekeeper, Cecil Holmes. What transpired was to change my life. 'Holmes', he said, 'I

Cecil Holmes with dogs

want you to take this boy out every day and look after him'. From that day, come sunshine or shower, and whatever the tasks of the day, I spent my time quietly looking and learning from the best teacher that a boy could ever have had.

December and January are particularly busy times for gamekeepers. There were one or two (English) partridge shoots and four or five pheasant shoots at Loudham each winter, and these were generally regarded as opportunities for the keeper to 'show' his birds to the best of his ability. Syndicates that paid were then unknown and the only money that changed hands were the tips that were pressed into the gamekeeper's hand after the last drive of the afternoon, when a couple of brace of birds were put in each gun's car.

I soon learned that a successful day's shooting entailed a lot of organization. Holmes would discuss with Uncle Denis on the previous day the format for each drive and whether or not it was 'cocks only'. Depending on the direction of the wind, pegs needed to be put out beforehand to indicate where each gun was to stand. Holmes would also liaise with the bailiff over the provision of beaters and pickers up. Each of these earned five shillings, and the chance of taking a rabbit or pheasant home at the end of the day. At each drive the beaters would line up, with Holmes and his dogs in the centre, awaiting the whistle blast which would be the key for them to advance slowly forward, tapping trees or making blood-curdling noises to encourage the birds to take to the wing. At the extreme ends of the line would be one man with a flag to discourage birds from breaking to the right, and another, with the same task, on the left.

The guns were all friends of my guardians and, for the most part, first rate shots. Most birds were killed cleanly, but at the end of each drive the guns would indicate to the pickers-up the location of any runners or dead birds that had fallen some way behind them. The whole operation was run like a military exercise, there was very little suffering and most birds were quickly accounted for. Inevitably, a handful needed finding and picking up the following morning and I would help in this operation with Holmes and his well-trained dogs. The average bag was never more than a hundred and fifty.

It was while I was still in my twenties that I was lucky enough to have a number of days shooting in Scotland, either along the foreshore of the River Nith near Dumfries, or at Slains in Aberdeenshire. Flighting geese in the early morning is quite unlike any other forms of shooting. After rising long before dawn and stumbling through the uneven ground by torchlight, one finally selects a suitable place to hide behind a bank or stone wall, and there one awaits the first distant cry of hundreds of wild geese flighting in from the sea against the pink light of dawn. Gradually the noise becomes louder as skein after skein passes overhead. Sometimes one never gets a chance of a shot. On one particular occasion a pair of greylag flew towards me and I fired both barrels. The first was a clean miss and the second shot brought one bird down, winged, in a marshy spot a good three hundred yards behind me in a place that was quite inaccessible. To make matters worse, its mate, hearing its cry, circled round it twice and then landed close beside it. Their distress was all too clear. And that was the end of my gamebird shooting.

Being with Holmes every day during the school holidays enabled me gradually to learn how to set snares and gin traps – the latter, thankfully, now illegal – to identify the tracks of weasels, foxes and hedgehogs, to make and mend purse nets and long nets, both of which were in constant use against rabbits, and to gut and skin a variety of animals. Moles were not easy to trap but, with practice, I gradually got fairly proficient, and mole skins, at threepence a piece, were a useful addition to my pocket money.

The river Deben, which ran through the farm, was full of a variety of coarse fish – roach, perch, bream and so on – and Holmes helped me to make my first fishing rod, using bamboo, twine, ping pong ball for a float, and hooks costing a penny a piece from a shop in Wickham Market. The mill race held eels, some of them weighing up to three or four pounds and we caught these in wire netting traps lowered into the water. Eels seemed to be most active at night, so we often got a pleasant surprise on pulling the traps up first thing in the morning. I remember once grabbing a good size eel from the trap, holding it by the tail and knocking its head as hard as I could against a post. I noticed one of the cowmen watching.

'Yew won't kill 'un tha' a'way, boi', he said. 'Eelce only die when yew knock'un on the tail'.

The life history of the eel is remarkable. All sorts of theories abounded until the year 1985, when it was finally proved that they start life in the Sargasso Sea, some four to seven thousand miles from the various parts of Europe and North Africa where they are destined to live their adult lives. The larvae, which are at first transparent, take three years to cross the Atlantic and swim into the various brackish waters and rivers where they feed on mussels, snails and a variety of other small fish. After anything between five and ten years of age they start the return journey to where they themselves began life, an area that in places is three miles deep. There, it is assumed that, after spawning, they die, but to this day no adult eel or egg has ever been found in the Sargasso Sea.

Thanks to Holmes, who seemed to know the names and nesting habits of all the birds that we encountered, my own knowledge gradually increased. This was helped a lot when, on my first Christmas at Loudham I became the proud owner of the *Observer's Book of Birds*. Then, once I reached the age of nine or ten, I was allowed to lie on the floor in Uncle Denis's smoking room and spend many happy hours looking through page after page of his set of the large edition of *British Birds* by the incomparable Archibald Thorburn.

From my earliest childhood I have always been fascinated by butterflies and moths, and I will be eternally grateful to another of Uncle Denis's close friends for the help and encouragement that he gave me. This was Alec Douglas-Home, another excellent cricketer in his day and destined to become one of our prime ministers. My uncle used to spend the latter part of August each year staying with him at The Hirsel, in Berwickshire, where he had several days' grouse shooting. The roles were then reversed, when A. D.-H. came and stayed with us at Loudham, where he would take me to the fields of lucerne most afternoons. There I used to catch clouded yellows, pale clouded yellows, silver-washed fritillaries and other exciting butterfly species, all of which are now sadly much reduced in numbers.

A short distance from the house was the horse pond and beside that stood a magnificent old elm tree. Only a stone's throw from the elm was a small apple orchard containing Aunt Madeline's favourite apples – Cox's Orange Pippins and Blenheim Oranges. In the summer holidays there were always windfall apples lying on the ground, many of which had started to rot, and this was where we found Large Tortoiseshell butterflies feasting on the rotting fruit. A. D.-H. encouraged me to try and breed this species by throwing sticks up into the elm tree to dislodge the caterpillars which feed on the leaves. I remember that some of these caterpillars were dead or dying, and he explained to me that Large Tortoiseshell caterpillars were particularly susceptible to attacks by parasitic ichneumon flies. These creatures inject their eggs into their hosts' bodies, where the resulting grubs proceed to feed on the flesh of the unfortunate larvae before emerging as flies. Large Tortoiseshells were a fairly common species then in southern Britain, but were brought to the verge of extinction by the effects of Dutch Elm disease on its main food plant. Since 1951 there have been less than a hundred and fifty sightings, but these have been mainly on the south and east coasts of Britain and are almost certainly migrants from the continent or releases of captive-bred stock. It is now generally considered to be extinct in Britain, so it can only be hoped that migrant numbers will increase and take hold and that the situation can be reversed.

A. D.-H. also told my aunt that, next time she took me to London, she was to make sure we visited number thirty-six, The Strand. When I asked him what we would find there he just grinned and said 'Wait and see'. It wasn't until just before Christmas in 1942, when my kind Aunt Madeline combined a visit to see Father Christmas at Harrods with my first introduction to a firm called Watkins & Doncaster, then owned and run by Richard Ford, a well-known entomologist. As soon as we opened the door, there in front of me lay a whole Pandora's box of wonderful things – butterfly nets of various sizes, setting boards, cabinets and framed boxes of large iridescent blue butterflies which Mr. Ford told me were morphos, from South America. A whole hour later I came out proudly clutching my first storage box (a welcome advance from pinning butterflies into notebooks), two volumes of South's *Moths of the British Isles* – I already had the companion book on butterflies – and a smelly concoction for painting onto posts or tree trunks to attract moths. As soon as the weather got warmer, I followed the instructions and began learning about another group of insects, many of which were just as large and as colourful as the butterflies. Over seventy-five years later I still buy things from Watkins & Doncaster, currently located in Kent and owned by Amy, Richard Ford's grand-daughter.

Now, on that happy note, it is time to move the clock forward to the time when, as a grown-up student, I went back to school for a year to learn about modern methods of farming.

(Nearest camera) Uncle Denis, Aunt Madeline, Eila (*c.* 1949)

Yet More Learning

I had always wanted to farm and, when I left the army, had accordingly decided to enrol on a one-year course at the Royal Agricultural College (now a university) in Cirencester. I had been brought up on an old-fashioned farm in East Anglia, where I had spent most of my time during school holidays either rough shooting, milking the cows and goats, or helping Cecil Holmes, the gamekeeper, with the many tasks that he had to do. One of these was looking after a couple of hives of bees and providing honey for the house. Beekeeping bore little resemblance then to its modern equivalent. If metal smokers (to calm the bees) were around in the early 1940s, we never saw them; nor did we use any protective veils, gloves or bee suits. In place of smokers Cecil would go down on his hands and knees in front of each hive and puff a little smoke from his Woodbine cigarette into the entrance. For my part I soon learned that if I made any sudden or rough movement it would frighten the bees and, not surprisingly, they would respond by stinging me. Beekeeping was probably a little easier and safer in those days. The bees we were working with then were good old native English bees, not very productive but generally pretty docile. After the war, with the aim of increasing honey production, queen bees were imported from Italy and from New Zealand. Pure native English bees are now reduced to a very few colonies, living in the wild and very susceptible to disease. The 'foreigners' work very hard, bring in a lot of honey, but can be a bit temperamental.

The farm itself was run on very different lines to those of today. Shooting, starting with partridges on the first of September, was one of the priorities, and any other activity was frequently regarded as of lesser importance. It was a 'mixed' farm, so we had dual-purpose Red Poll cattle, a number of Large White pigs, and I remember that Baldrey, the pigman, only used his teeth when it was time to castrate any piglets. On this and many other farms tractors only came in towards the end of the war, and before that we used Suffolk Punches for ploughing and most other heavy tasks. 'Drawing a furrow' in an unwavering straight line was a real test for both horse and ploughman, and I well remember how proud I was at coming third in the boys' contest at the Woodbridge Horse Show. The arable farming was based on the four-year rotation system, originally designed by 'Turnip' Townshend in Norfolk around 1730. This in his case consisted of turnips (hence his nickname), then a cereal crop (wheat, oats, rye or barley), then one year fallow (leaving the land uncultivated), then either a second cereal crop or grass for grazing. My recollection is that in place of turnips we grew other crops, particularly swedes for cattle fodder in the winter, or kale, excellent pheasant cover and also feed for the cattle.

When harvest was over, the stubble was never ploughed in until well into the New Year, and generous headlands provided plenty of food for partridges and other birds. Herbicides were never used, and muck from the horses, cattle and pigsties were the only fertilizers. The average size of each arable field was about three or four acres, and our total acreage, I remember, was about thirteen hundred, much of which was woodland and water meadows.

The labour force amounted to ten or a dozen men, often related and answerable to a bailiff. He (Robinson) wore riding breeches and boots and sported a gold watch on the end of a chain. The average farm worker's wage in 1942 was £4–£5 a week, and a loaf of bread cost eight old pence.

Farm cottages were supplied to all the workers, but proper sanitation and electric lighting were things of the future. Children walked unattended, whatever the weather, to the local school which was about a mile from the farm. Sexual misbehaviour towards young girls or boys was unheard of. Minor crimes, including poaching, were dealt with summarily by the local policeman. The culprit would usually finish up with a few bruises and a black eye. Nobody complained, and this form of rough justice was very effective. As a boy I remember the endless laughter, the jokes and the light-hearted leg-pulling, often directed at me, although I was always addressed as 'Master Iain'. (I remember, to my amusement, that when I came back to the farm as a newly commissioned subaltern, aged nineteen, I was still 'Master Iain'. This only changed when I was eventually promoted to 'Captain Iain' and then 'Major Iain').

The climax to the farming year was always the completion of the harvest. Cutting the corn was carried out very slowly, starting round the headlands and then proceeding rotationally inwards. When only a small area was left, this was the signal for all the young, the local policeman, the butcher and all the womenfolk, armed with stout ash sticks, to position themselves round the remaining area and wait for the rabbits to bolt. Some of these rabbits made it safely to the neighbouring woodland, while others took refuge under nearby sheaves. With much laughter and screaming, half a dozen youths would pounce on these sheaves and, accompanied by much ribaldry, the rabbit usually succeeded in bolting to safety between someone's legs.

When the harvest was all safely in, all the farm workers and their families were invited up to the Hall, where beer, cider and soft drinks were dispensed and everyone was thanked for their hard work. A similar gathering was also organised on Christmas Eve.

The Christmas stockings that my sister and I got were a far cry from what many children get nowadays. Ours always had an orange or tangerine in the toe (both were an imported luxury in wartime Britain), a packet of sweets (humbugs and barley sugar were our favourites), a paperback, a pack of cards and a diary. All these were treats for us in the 1940s, and I well remember the excitement of tasting my first banana at the end of the war. Christmas lunch, when we listened to the King's speech, consisted of turkey from the farm and plum pudding. Our two servants – Big Mary (who weighed about fourteen stone) and Little Mary (about twelve stone) were expected to serve lunch, wash up and then lay a cold supper for the family. At around four in the afternoon they went off to their families in Wickham Market, and were expected to be back at work by lunchtime the following day.

After Eila and I had been at Loudham for about five years we were allowed to have lunch downstairs with our guardians, and that was where, on most days, an interesting scenario used to be played out. Robinson, the foreman, had by then been retired, and in his place came Ernie Clack, a dapper little man who seemed to us to be far too full of himself and to spend an inordinate amount of his time in the servants' hall. On most days, after lunch, Aunt Madeline and Uncle Denis used to go for a walk, and on each of these occasions a prior discussion would have taken place, while the pudding plates were being removed by one of the Mary's, to agree to what part of the farm they would visit that afternoon. One day it would be Copperas, another day Park Farm, and so on. Whatever the destination, the details were, not surprisingly, transmitted to the servants' quarters where 'Cocky' Clack (as we called him) was almost invariably lurking. Forty minutes later he would step out from behind a shed, doff his cap, and it would be "afternoon Captain, 'afternoon Mrs. Wigan, beautiful day, isn't it', before telling them the latest news from that part of the farm. Many was the occasion when I heard my uncle, on his return to the house, say 'Marvellous man, Clack, he really does get round the place extremely thoroughly ...' Several years later, while I was undergoing national service in the army, 'Cocky' lived up to his name a bit too often. He put both Marys in the family way and, as a consequence, had to lose his job.

Rabbits were the chief vermin on the farm in the early days of my time at Loudham and Cecil and a few part-time volunteers, armed with long-nets, purse-nets, ferrets, gin traps and guns accounted for a thousand or more every year. Rabbit meat, so often scorned nowadays, was our staple diet during the war, only augmented during the shooting season with pheasant, partridge and sundry other game. Chicken was a treat. The vast population of rabbits also encouraged stoats and weasels, and harvest-time brought in a multitude of rats. Good sport used to be had then by groups of boys, armed with sticks, together with the keeper's terriers, around the stacks and the threshing floor. Very few rats survived this onslaught.

Birds regarded then as winged vermin included magpies, jays, crows, jackdaws, little owls and sparrowhawks. It is interesting here to look at the changing status of some species. I have in my library the author's annotated copy of Tuck's 'Ornithology of Suffolk', published in 1891. Julian Tuck was rector of Tostock, near Bury St. Edmunds and, like many rural parsons of his day, was a keen and observant naturalist. Surprisingly, he gives the status of the magpie as 'formerly bred: a stray pair may now nest occasionally'. And 'the little owl is now a very rare visitant'.

That the magpie was virtually extinct in Suffolk at that time seems, at first sight, almost unbelievable. That, however, was the period when East Anglia had a number of very large estates – Holkham, Elvedon, Houghton, Orwell Park, to name just a few – each with a whole covey of gamekeepers, whose number one job was vermin control. Yes, the Good Lord created the magpie and made it an inveterate egg-stealer, but I do not know of anyone who would be happy if this flashy, black and white member of the avian kingdom was lost to us for ever.

The case of the little owl is rather different. A lot of people believed that they only killed the odd gamebird so they could feed on their main diet of carrion beetles that go to the corpses. That argument, however, went unheeded by the Victorian gamekeepers who brought them to the brink of extinction. Then, starting around 1888, the eminent ornithologist, Lord Lilford, and several other landowners, concerned by the plight of the little owl in Britain, organized importations from mainland Europe where the species was plentiful. Still the argument continued as to whether or not little owls were harmful to gamebirds. It was not until 1936 and 1937 that two investigations were commissioned by the British Trust for Ornithology. Thousands of little owl pellets from around the country were examined, many from areas where there were poultry farms or shooting estates. Two interesting facts emerged. One, in the whole two-year investigation, only one certain and one doubtful game-chick and seven poultry chicks were found in the pellets. Secondly, the canard that little owls kill purely in order to attract beetles was disproved, for carrion beetles only formed a very small total in the analyses. What was proved conclusively was that little owls feed on insects, rodents, birds and a few amphibians. Earwigs, interestingly, outnumbered all other components of their diet.

I was under no illusions that farming methods in the 1960s would bear little resemblance to those of the 1940s. Whereas my childhood memories were of a need, in those wartime days, to maximize crop yields within the constraints of the time, this was very seldom done to the detriment of the land or nature. It would, instinctively, have been sacrilege to have dug out hedges that had been there for hundreds of years, or to have ploughed up wetlands with all their interesting wildflowers, and bird life.

It is not easy to attempt to analyse these memories of years gone by, but I suppose that we and all those around us in the 1940s were instinctively trying to do our best to maintain the balance of nature. There was no word for it then, but the modern word of course is 'conservation'. It is often said, and I believe it to be true that by and large sportsmen, with very few exceptions, are and always have been the best conservationists in the country.

Certainly, Cirencester came as a big shock. The key phrase, which was repeated in almost all our lectures, was the Gross Margin Analysis System, or how much money you could make from each acre. Yes, it stood to reason that if you grubbed out three old hedges around several adjoining small fields, and made one much bigger field, it would be better for your machinery and increase your crop size. Also, if you cultivated up to

Constable painting of Daws Hall, c. 1800

the extreme edges of this new field, your yields would be improved even more. And water meadows, what was the point of them, with their wonderful rich soil untapped? Plough them up and yet another grant was available. How ironic to think that now, after so much irreparable damage has been done, government grants are available for leaving broad headlands, restoring hedges and leaving fields fallow. The majority of water meadows, alas, have gone for good.

Cirencester, of course, was not all lectures. Gloucestershire social life was pretty hectic and thoroughly enjoyable, and d'Esterre and I made many new friends. However, I must confess that I came away not really wanting to become an arable farmer. Yes, I wanted a life on the land, but it had to be something out of the ordinary. We went up to Norfolk and I fell in love with a wonderful unspoilt Broad – 300 acres of reedbeds, marsh harriers, bearded tits and bitterns – but d'Esterre understandably put her foot down and the dream died a death.

Finally, we settled on a wildfowl farm on the Suffolk/Essex border, and the story of this venture has been told by me in two earlier books, *Flying Feathers*, 1977, and its sequel *Ruffled Feathers*, 1978. What has never been told until now has been, first, the creation of an environmental education centre and nature reserve for the benefit of local schoolchildren; and, secondly, my amateurish attempts to establish a small arboretum and garden which will hopefully be used and appreciated by those who come after us.

Arrival at Daws Hall

I quite often make a fool of myself and there was one particular day in the late autumn of 1965 that was no exception. We had just agreed to buy Daws Hall – part Tudor, part Georgian, with sixteen acres of land – and I was walking round the house with the previous owner who was kindly pointing out various things that she felt we ought to know. In the middle of the lawn was an old mulberry tree, which I was in fact able to recognize because there was a similar one in the garden at Loudham. It was then that I spotted a curious looking plant growing up the front of the house. It was covered in scarlet berries.

'Gosh', I said, 'what is that?'

'That is a cotoneaster', came her reply.

I rapidly pulled out the small notebook and pencil that I always carry, wrote down the name, and made a mental note to order half a dozen of these amazing looking shrubs.

'Is it very rare?' I asked.

'No, it is actually extremely common', she said, and I thought I detected a rather pitying look in my direction.

That was in fact my introduction to gardening in England. Yes, we had had a garden in Uganda, and were actually quite proud of the small collection of bougainvillea – one a present from Pinky Jackson – frangipanis, oleanders and other tropical plants that we had managed to assemble. Obviously, on the Suffolk/ Essex border I had a lot to learn.

Also, not far from the house, there was a large tree. She saw where I was looking and told me that it was a tulip tree, explaining that the flowers, resembling those of tulips, normally appear around the middle of June.

'I'm afraid this particular tree', she said, 'has not had any flowers at all for the past six or seven years. You might like to think about cutting it down and starting again. It's had a good innings, probably two hundred years or so. New trees should flower after about twenty or twenty-five years'.

Although I knew nothing whatever about tulip trees, this did seem to me a little drastic. Anyway, the following week I looked up 'tree surgeons' in my *Yellow Pages*. There were three or four listed, one of whom had the very apt name of Mr. Sycamore, and he agreed to come and have a look at it the following afternoon. 'Well, Mr. Sycamore', I said, after he had spent a good half hour inspecting the tree from all angles, 'do we need to cut it down?'

Our 300-year-old tulip tree and a flower

'Cu' it down? Certainly not, booi', came the reply in his rich Suffolk accent. 'A big job, though, tak' a good two days, but she'll be roight as rain when o'ive finished on'er'.

We agreed a price and one week later he started. 'She be a dern sight too top'eavy', he explained, before climbing up with remarkable agility for a man of his sixty-odd years. The chain-saw whirred and soon a lot of the higher branches came crashing down. One look at the rotten wood and I began to see why the tree hadn't flowered for so long.

Having reduced the tree to about two thirds of its original height, he started to attack it at ground level. I went off to do another job and, next time I saw him, he had almost disappeared inside the tree.

'Rotten as a rotten egg, booi', he explained, as he filled yet another barrow-load of decaying timber.

Satisfied with his day's work, Mr. Sycamore departed. Rather to my surprise, when I saw him the following morning, I noticed that he had ordered a delivery of Ready-mix, which he was proceeding to shovel into the base of my poor, long-suffering tree.

'You do know what you're doing, do you, Mr. Sycamore?' I said, rather nervously.

'Course oi knows what oi'se doin', booi', came the well-deserved retort, and after that I kept my mouth shut.

A couple of years later we had our first tulip tree flowers, and every year since then the wonderful display has reappeared. A little light surgery was in fact needed recently to some of the topmost branches, but the tree surgeon who did the work knew of Mr. Sycamore – sadly now no longer – and said he was 'a legend'.

Scything was one of the skills that I learnt as a boy and I was delighted to find that I had not forgotten this dying art. In fact I remember cutting two acres of hay and feeling remarkably fresh at the end of the day. Too many people either use brute force, or keep rotating the body through 180 degrees, or both. The first rule to successful scything is keep the scythe razor-sharp by stopping and using the 'stone' every ten minutes or so. Secondly, start each stroke of the scythe from a position immediately in front of you, then draw the scythe in one smooth, unhurried stroke towards the left hand side of your midriff. (If you've watched Poldark on TV, he does everything diametrically opposite!).

Many are the mistakes that I've made in my life, but if there is one sensible thing I've done it is to plant trees. It is an occupation I can recommend to anyone who is fortunate enough to own a plot of land.

My advice to those who want to build up a little collection of trees, or indeed to plant an arboretum, is to go and see as many similar establishments as you can. Talk to the owners, who will almost always be happy to offer advice, and always make notes. You will spot good ideas, you will see the opposite, and both impressions, I believe, are equally important.

I was extremely fortunate, when I started gardening, getting to know the now legendary Beth Chatto, whose world-famous garden at Elmstead Market, near Colchester, is less than an hour's drive from my home. I remember on one particular occasion going to see her shortly after I had embarked on buying and planting my first half dozen or so unusual trees. I could not help but notice that young trees of hers, also recently planted, were doing much better than mine. I asked her why, and she smiled and said 'well, you probably don't know how to plant them'.

'O.K., Beth, I'm sure you're right. Do, please, give me your advice'.

That was fifty years ago and I shall never forget her reply: 'When I want my gardeners to plant a tree here, I tell them to dig a hole deep enough to bury an elephant'.

I looked at her, mouth open and somewhat flabbergasted, but gradually I could see what she meant. Nobody is going to dig a hole that deep, but what she believed to be crucial was to dig a hole, the deeper the better, and fill it with as much and as many nutrients as possible – well-rotted leaf mould and horse muck, garden compost and so on. Experts argue incessantly over whether the hole should be round, square, or some other abstruse shape, but I have always tried to follow her simple, sound advice. There have been many occasions over the years when visitors to this garden cannot believe the true age of some of our trees.

Among the trees that I planted then, which can be seen and appreciated by visitors to the garden now, are the following. The first two of these are now taller than our four-hundred-year-old cedar of Lebanon.

Abies grandis – Giant fir
Sequoia sempervirens – Coastal redwood
Fagus sylvatica Dawyck – Dawyck beech
Liriodendron tulipifera aureomarginatum – Variegated tulip tree
Acer maximowiczianum– Nikko maple
Cupressus macrocarpa – Monterey cypress
Acer cappadocicum aureum – Golden Cappadocian maple
Acer palmatum Osakazuki (probably the best for autumn colour)
Malus tschonoskii – Pillar apple
Betula szechuanika – Szechuan birch.

I well remember another visit to her garden one day in the month of May. Her famous 'gravel garden' was taking shape, but what caught my eye was a tree with no sign of any leaves on it, but with a profusion of blue foxglove-shaped flowers. I had never seen anything like it. Beth was working not far away and she told me it was a foxglove tree, Latin name *Paulownia tomentosa*. Nowadays the worldwide internet enables one to track down almost anything that is growing in the furthest reaches of the globe, but back in the early 1970s this service had not yet become available. It took me another two or three years before I eventually found one for sale. The usual deep hole was dug in a sheltered corner of the garden and the young tree responded with gusto. After six or seven years we had our first blue flowers and, better still, a strong-looking root sucker

Paulownia flowers

emerged from the ground about five yards from the mother tree. This we dug up during the dormant season and in that way we had our second foxglove tree for free. They are the fastest growing trees that I know but, alas, they are also the fastest dying. Our original parent tree died when it was thirty-five years old and her daughter when she was twenty-eight.

The habit of paulownias to push out root suckers does in fact give them a whole new dimension. Here we wait until the suckers are about five or six foot high and then, in February, we cut them down to their base. This results in rapid and phenomenal growth, and by the autumn it is not unusual to have stems five or six metres tall and leaves measuring eighty centimetres across. This process can seemingly continue indefinitely. The older the sucker, the more stems it throws out, but my advice is continue coppicing them in February, but cut out and discard all bar the strongest three at the most.

Our soil here is neutral to slightly acid and fairly light, with an overall *pH* measurement of around 5.5 or 6.0. Good shelter from strong winds is essential and very young trees can occasionally succumb to severe frost. The attractive paulownia genus, with around six or seven species, hails from eastern Asia. The rarest of these is *P. kawakamii*, from the island of Taiwan, and reputably limited to no more than a hundred trees left in the wild. This exceptionally beautiful species, of which there is a splendid example at Kew, is particularly susceptible to frost when it is still in its early days. A young tree in this garden flowered when it was seven years old in 2018 and looks in good heart as I write.

Like many aspiring gardeners and tree lovers (or dendrologists to give them their smart name), I gradually became part of a small circle of like-minded friends, owners of garden centres, botanists and others, where ideas, experiences and plants are constantly exchanged to the general benefit of all. As with most gardeners I soon became interested in particular groups of trees and shrubs and started to add some of these to the collection. The acers (or maples) number well over a hundred different species in the wild, with innumerable garden forms or cultivars. Many of these are at their showiest in the autumn when their leaves of scarlet, orange and yellow lighten up the whole garden. This to me is a particularly exciting time of the year, when our cornuses (dogwoods), nyssas and liquidambars are all at their best.

Anyway, time now to leave the garden, with all its changing moods and colours, and to turn to something which had long been an ambition of mine – the creation of a nature reserve and education centre for young people in Essex and Suffolk.

OVERLEAF The author with paulownia suckers after one year's growth

The First Schoolchildren Arrive

As with the garden, I was fortunate in meeting the right people and having help at the right time. One of these, David, was a regular golfing companion of mine and, as luck would have it, he was then head of the education department of the local council. Robbie, also a good friend, was an all-round naturalist and at that time chairman of the local wildlife society. Somehow he had got to hear that we had a breeding pair of red-backed shrikes on our land, and used to come over, enjoy a glass of malt whisky and photograph this rapidly declining species.

The three of us held an initial meeting, armed with a variety of alcoholic beverages. I had recently purchased a little extra land, including an unspoilt strip bordering the River Stour and a four acre field on which I had planted native oak and beech with a nurse crop of Scot's pine. All of this, I remember, cost me the princely sum of a hundred pounds an acre at a time when good agricultural land, as I remember from my Cirencester days, was changing hands for up to two thousand pounds an acre.

After a couple of hours we had the framework of an agreement. I offered to provide the land and find the money to convert my garage into a simple education centre. David said he would arrange for the council to provide and pay the salaries of a full-time environmental education teacher, plus part-time secretarial assistance, and also to get the council to build me a replacement garage. Robbie, who was thrilled to have found below my new wood what turned out to be one of the strongest sites in Essex of native yellow rattle *Rhinanthus minor*, together with a botanical rarity, the narrow-leaved water dropwort *Oenanthe silaifolia*, was in an expansive mood. He promised to provide all the technical and scientific advice and help that we might need. By the end of the evening the framework of this new venture was beginning to take shape.

For my part I had to honour my side of the agreement. Two thousand five hundred pounds, a tidy sum in those days, was the quotation provided by the local builder for doing the necessary conversions to my old garage, which had been, in its day, originally a coach house, and then much later an incubator room and a pigsty. I reckoned that I had close on a hundred public-spirited friends in the area who, if properly approached, might be persuaded to each part with twenty-five pounds. A pleading letter was sent by me to each of them, explaining what I had in mind and, to my amazement, almost all of them sent me a cheque for the required amount. Some actually sent me double, and one kind person gave me two hundred and fifty pounds. The best part for me, however, were the letters of encouragement that I received, together with the realization that this project was indeed something worthwhile and one that could benefit local schoolchildren and the local community.

↑ Converting my garage into a schoolroom

↑ More than 20 small tortoiseshell butterflies on a sedum. A common sight in the 1980s but, sadly, no longer

While work started on the garage conversion, Robbie came over once more and, with his help, we mapped out the various significant areas that were required on the reserve. A wildflower meadow was needed, and for this we had an ideal site – a three-acre field of unimproved pasture and light soil. Here I could not help but cast my mind back to the days of my own childhood, when flower-rich meadows were everywhere, teeming with butterflies, grasshoppers and day-flying moths, and when herbicides and chemical fertilizers were virtually unknown.

Fortunately, Robbie was on hand to tell me how to prepare the ground. With his help and that of a local farmer we started by spraying the meadow with Round-up on three separate occasions, in April, July and October. By then everything growing on the field was dead. In November the farmer came back and scattered a seed-mix of local wildflowers and non-aggressive grasses which we had obtained from a specialist supplier. He finished the operation with a couple of passes of a Cambridge roller.

'Too many people', Robbie explained, 'try and create a flower meadow on land that is too rich. If you've got nettles and thistles, you've got the wrong site. Another mistake people make is to use a plough or a rotovator. If you do this, you are bringing to the surface seeds of plants you don't want that have lain dormant for hundreds of years'.

An area of woodland was also needed and here at least I had made a start with my four acres of native hardwood. On top of this we already had quite a number of mature oak, ash, poplar, pine and so on, so what was urgently required were some fast-growing shrubs, such as sallow, hawthorn, spindle, dog rose and blackthorn. Robbie kindly offered to provide a number of these for free, together with some volunteers to plant and fence them.

Water is of course a vital element on any nature reserve and, where children are involved, it is important to have 'dipping areas', where they can safely catch, examine and then release the various different freshwater invertebrates that they have found. We

The scene in our wildflower meadow during the first couple of years when it was dominated by ox-eye daisies

From: Sir Peter Scott CH CBE DSC FRS

THE NEW GROUNDS
SLIMBRIDGE
GLOUCESTER GL2 7BS

Tel: Cambridge (Glos.) (045-389) 333

17th January, 1989

Dear Iain

I would be happy to be quoted in your appeal brochure in the following words:

The Daws Hall Trust is doing most valuable work in introducing large numbers of school children to the plants and animals in a beautiful unspoilt part of the country. The Trust gives children a wonderful opportunity to learn at first hand, both to enjoy wildlife and how important it is to conserve a variety of habitats.

Yours ever

Peter

Major Iain Grahame.

Letter from Sir Peter Scott, January 1989

Ted Ellis opening our schoolroom, 1 Nov. 1985. George Carrick, our first teacher is on the left, next to David, who did so much to help us in the early days (photo EADT)

Gainsborough stood on what is now our land when he painted this distant scene of Sudbury. The steep bank, which was formed during the Second Ice Age, some 20,000 years ago, is now home to several families of badgers

already had a small stretch of the river Stour, plus the Losh-house Brook, a tributary that flows into it. We now planned a separate area, using water that overflowed from the duck ponds that I had created on the wildfowl farm. This we called the 'scrape', and the hope was that it would encourage sandpipers, snipe and so on, together with marginal wildflowers.

A lot of work was clearly going to be needed and, by luck, a new government-funded project, the Manpower Services Scheme, had just started. Our application was duly approved, and Trevor, Graeme and Martin, three unemployed young men from Sudbury, started work here the following month. Apart from one of them falling into the river and another stepping on a wasp nest, everything went smoothly. Not only did they enjoy their time here, but by the end of the year they were all beginning to learn quite a lot about nature.

After these three we had Paul the Coffin. Why coffin? Well, I can see it to this day, his motorcycle complete with side-car. Nothing unusual about that, except for the fact that his side-car consisted of a converted coffin, in which his long-suffering girlfriend was forced to travel on outings to the cinema. Anyway, thanks to the hard work of these Manpower Services lads and the continued support that we had from Robbie, David and their respective organizations, the development of the new reserve proceeded according to plan. Mown paths round the various sectors, each with its own ecological signifi-cance, marked out the nature trails for use by visiting schools. A grand opening was conducted by a good friend and delightful Norfolk naturalist, Ted Ellis in 1985, and, to my delight, schools soon began to come here on a regular basis. Three years later we were granted charitable status and the Daws Hall Trust came into being.

Most children are charming, but just a few, in varying degrees, can be utterly odious. Take the case of Kevin, who came with his classmates to our nature reserve many years ago. As far as I know he never mugged old ladies or tortured little kittens, but Kevin's form of pestilentiousness was far more direct and straightforward. To the endless despair of his parents and his teachers, he would never do what he was asked to do; in fact he took pleasure in doing the opposite. Rules or instructions were stubbornly ignored, and any form of reprimand was greeted, at best with sullen indifference, at worst with a glare of undiluted hatred.

On the day in question a group of schoolchildren, including Kevin, were walking through the wood when our teacher spotted an owl 'pellet'. Much to everyone's surprise a little voice piped up. 'Please, sir, may I hold it?' It was Kevin, and the teacher, a little surprised, readily agreed. Until they adjourned for lunch in the classroom Kevin could be seen, totally absorbed in this object that had recently been disgorged by one of our resident tawny owls. And the story doesn't end there. While the other children were tucking in to their packed lunches Kevin went off to the furthest corner of the classroom. There he took the owl pellet to pieces and proceeded, with infinite care, to reconstruct the skeleton of a vole.

A week or so later the telephone rang. It was Kevin's father, telling me that his son had changed out of all recognition. He had become utterly absorbed in the natural world, and his parents were doing all they could to encourage this new-found interest.

Much of the success or otherwise of these school visits depends, inevitably, on the calibre of our teaching staff, and here we have been extremely fortunate. George, Matt, Richard and Sarah have all in their different ways been first class, and after them we had Simon. Not only did he have a natural aptitude for teaching children of all ages, but he was an excellent all-round naturalist. We were indeed fortunate to have had him. He and Sarah, his wife, retired to the West Country in 2017 after being in charge here for close on thirty years. We now have the delightful Amy, who is excellent with children and appears to enjoy this place as much as we enjoy having her.

Many years have now passed since Kevin's reconstruction of the vole, and over a hundred thousand children have been here on educational visits. Each year, on selected days, we open the reserve and the gardens to the general public. Frequently children arrive clearly longing to show their parents some particular area – maybe a corner of the woodland, maybe the dipping ponds – where they had found some fascinating bug or beast on a recent school trip. Even more rewarding for us is when parents of visiting families come and tell us of the fond memories that they have of their time spent here

Simon Perry

when they themselves were children. One day – who knows? – one of these fathers might introduce himself as Kevin.

How many of the children who come here experience a life-changing experience like Kevin, I will of course never know. What I do know is that only a tiny proportion of today's young grasp the opportunities that my generation had. Living in the country, long before the days of computer games and other such diversions, I was encouraged, whatever the weather, to go outside and explore. Scratched knees and soaking clothes were a small price to pay for the joy of watching a stoat hypnotise a rabbit before jumping in for the kill, or discovering a nightingale's nest deep inside a thicket. These simple delights and country pursuits taught me much more than gawping for hours on end at a television screen or mobile telephone that do nothing more than encourage total vacuity of the adolescent human brain.

I think there must have been a bit of vacuity of the human brain one day shortly after I had purchased the extra bit of land bordering the Stour. The telephone rang and it was an earnest-sounding young man from Anglian Water Authority.

'I wonder whether I could come and see you', he said. 'One of our engineers has come up with a brainwave aimed at eliminating the regular flooding that occurs on a large stretch of the river. We wanted to have your reaction, not only as a conservationist, but also as one of the landowners that will be affected'.

Children on one of our dipping platforms

He came along that afternoon, and told me that the scheme they had in mind was to fill in the existing river along the four mile stretch between Sudbury and Bures, and then create a new straight waterway. 'You know, just like a canal', he added, as he saw the look of utter horror and astonishment on my face.

Mercifully, this 'brainwave' never progressed, but what they did do, despite strong opposition from me, was to build hideous embankments along much of this stretch of the river. To create these they had to excavate valuable reedbeds and their accompanying flora and fauna which, fifty years later, have still not fully recovered. The banks did indeed act as a barrier against minor flooding, but of course the big floods went over the top and the water was then unable to recede as it had done for centuries. John Constable must have been turning in his grave.

OVERLEAF View from our stretch of the Stour looking upstream towards Sudbury. The dreadful embankments can be seen in the middle distance on the left-hand side of the river

DAWS HALL
NATURE RESERVE

11 Stour Cliff
This steep slope provides views of the river and valley. The extensive digging in the soft sand is an established badger home or sett. Shallow scrapes made by badgers searching for worms can be found throughout the site.

7 Rattle Meadow
This is a small remnant of old waterside meadow and is the only remaining local site for yellow rattle. Look for the effect it has on grass growth during spring as this semi-parasitic yellow flowered plant obtains nutrition from the roots of grasses.

Yellow rattle

6 Chestnut Coppice
A small copse of sweet chestnut with different areas cut in rotation. The regenerating stumps create a mosaic of trees at various stages of development, providing a wide variety of habitats for ground flora and fauna.

Speckled wood butterfly

Losh House

Rattle Meadow

Chestnut Coppice ☒ ⑥

Lamarsh Hill Wood ⑤

5 Lamarsh Hill Wood
An arable field until the 1960s, and originally planted with Scots pine, beech and oak, this wood now has a developing understory including hazel, maple, ash and hawthorn. Glades have been created to provide warm sheltered sites for woodland plants and butterflies including speckled wood, comma and red admiral.

Red campion

④

③

3 Wild Flower Meadow
Sown with local seed and managed for wild flowers and invertebrates, this field is grazed by sheep during the winter and cut in late summer. The Meadow now boasts over 100 plant species and a variety of smaller animals.

Birdsfoot-trefoil

②

①
Centre

Daws
Hall

Common lizard

Meadow brown butterfly

8 Pitmire Plantation

The cricket bat willow trees planted here on the flood plain are gradually being removed. Now sown with wetland species and managed to encourage the spread of plants like ladies smock, large bitter cress and common valerian.

Common valerian

9 Pitmire Island and Lock

Still visible are the remains of the now derelict wooden lock, which was part of the navigation from Sudbury to the sea.

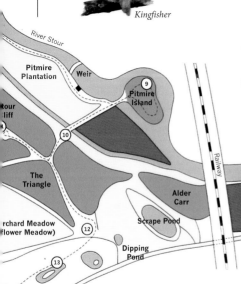

Kingfisher

N

River Stour

Pitmire
Plantation

Weir

9 Pitmire
Island

tour
liff

10

The
Triangle

Alder
Carr

Scrape Pond

rchard Meadow
flower Meadow)

12

Dipping
Pond

13

e
uary

Railway

Female

Male

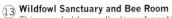

Banded demoiselle

Scrape Pond and Alder Carr

Originally excavated as a scrape for waterfowl and waders this pond is now especially good for water invertebrates including damselflies and dragonflies. Because it is so shallow it needs regular dredging to clear vegetation. An overflow drains into the marshy woodland area or carr.

13 14 Wildfowl Sanctuary and Bee Room

This area holds a collection of captive bred wildfowl. Many of the ducks and geese are free winged and can be seen flying over the reserve. During the spring and summer an observation beehive is maintained in the Bee Room.

Reedmace

Great spotted woodpecker

The Great Storm, 1987

Nobody who was in the eye of the Great Storm of 1987 will ever forget that experience. It was the most damaging weather event to hit the British Isles since 1703. The winds reached hurricane force, particularly in southern and eastern England and it was estimated that, in less than twenty-four hours, fifteen million trees were torn out of the ground. Not only trees, however, but power lines, roads, railways and houses were affected.

My first perception of it came at around five o'clock on the morning of 16 October. I was woken abruptly to the alarming sensation that the house was moving. Being an old house without foundations, this was exactly what was happening. One of my first thoughts was for my beloved tulip tree. I drew back the curtains. The hundred-year-old mulberry tree was lying on its side, in the middle of the lawn, with its roots in the air. Mercifully, the liriodendron appeared completely unscathed, and I offered a silent thank you to Mr. Sycamore. Further to the left, beside the duck pond, the cedar of Lebanon, a splendid old tree that had probably been planted around 1750, also appeared to be unharmed. Between the cedar and the tulip tree there was total devastation. A small copse of native oak and beech, numbering around 40 trees which were getting on for a hundred years old, together with a similar number of other trees, had all been hit by the eye of the storm.

I dressed, drank some badly needed coffee and went outside to assess what other damage there was. The young exotic trees that I had begun to plant had all, with one exception, survived pretty well. Rather like the mulberry, my fifteen-year-old *Sorbus mitchellii*, a lovely member of the rowan family with large rounded leaves that are whitish beneath, had been completely uprooted. As soon as I was able to assemble two strong helpers we winched the tree upright, cut off one big branch to balance the weight and gave it a good stake to keep it upright. Now, thirty years later, John Mitchell's sorbus stands proud, showing no sign of its horrendous experience in the Great Storm. On the reserve, all the young trees and shrubs had survived unscathed, and only a few old horse chestnuts and ash had been blown down.

The hurricane coincided with the end of Paul the Coffin's year with us, but the Scheme continued for a further year, and that was when Jonathan Clarke arrived. Unfazed by the fact that his one year was occupied almost entirely with clearing up after the hurricane, he applied to continue to work here on a long term contract. Over thirty years later he is still here, and all the many developments that have occurred during this time are largely due to his hard work, loyalty and perseverance.

16 Oct 1987 – scenes of total devastation

One of the reasons for the '87 Great Storm bringing down so many trees was that it came when they were still in full leaf and the ground in many areas was waterlogged. This was certainly the case in our small copse where the beeches, which are notorious for having a shallow rooting system, suffered a one hundred percent loss, and where only five of the oak trees survived. These five oaks, now about 150 years old, stand proud as the sole survivors of that dreadful storm.

OVERLEAF Cowslips in the Wild Flower Meadow in April

The task of clearing such a vast amount of debris, to say nothing of the cost, was so colossal that it took me a long time to recognize that anything good could conceivably come out of such adversity. Apart from the huge storm of 1703, others of almost equal intensity had occurred in 1792, 1825 and again in 1839. On each occasion vast numbers of trees would have been felled, but in this way nature would have presented a clean palette, enriched with years of rotted leaf mould, to whoever chose to benefit from these conditions. A year after the horrific events of 1987, and when the ground had finally been cleared, I began to notice the emergence of snowdrops, violets, and then wood anemones and primroses on the woodland floor. A soil check gave a reading of 5.5 *pH* – wonderful for acid-loving plants – and that is when I started with renewed enthusiasm to replant. Nyssas, a *Taxodium distichum* (swamp cypress), a eucryphia and several other rare or unusual trees and shrubs joined the embryonic collection. Dreams of starting a small arboretum gradually began to take shape.

The wildflower meadow was now well established and had become an increasingly important area for biodiversity studies, particularly by secondary school pupils. The mixture comprised a carefully selected variety of native species, and I was delighted to see the numbers and varieties of insects, particularly butterflies, that it attracted. Apart from the usual resident species, the meadow also regularly attracted migrants like the clouded yellow and the painted lady. At the end of the annual teaching season, normally

Blue and white scillas and narcissi

Chinodoxas and primroses on bank

some time in October, the meadow is mown and all the cuttings are collected and placed in a clamp where they gradually rot down and are used as compost.

Our ancestors valued wildflowers, but for very different reasons, namely their medicinal properties. The earliest references to these came in the first century AD with the appearance of *De Materia Medica* by a Greek author known today as Dioscorides. Fifteen hundred years later came the herbals of John Gerard, Thomas Johnson and Nicholas Culpepper, who were all early surgeons or apothecaries. Their herbals make interesting reading. For example, they tell us that the sap of comfrey was so strong it was used by the early physicians as a bone-setting agent, while the leaves of dandelion (or pissenlit in French) formed a valuable cure for urinary problems, and purple loosestrife was a popular wound cleaner or disinfectant. Another plant that was used as a remedy for urinary infections was lady's bedstraw, now widely distributed in our wildflower meadow. As the name implies its dried flowers were traditionally used for stuffing mattresses. Not only did the strong coumarin scent kill fleas, but it also apparently helped pregnant women to have a safe delivery. There is even a legend that Mary lay on a bedstraw mattress when giving birth to the infant Jesus. The cowslip was another plant associated with the Virgin Mary, with its local name of Mary's Tears. Here in East Anglia they are often called peggles, and they were widely believed to be a cure for cramp and insomnia. Culpeper claimed that an ointment of cowslip cream removed warts and wrinkles.

OVERLEAF The endangered Red-breasted Geese and a pair of Goldeneye

It was in the early 1990s that we had a visit from a lady from the council who was responsible for Health and Safety. We started by walking to the wildflower meadow, which had recently been cut and where half a dozen Hebridean ewes, borrowed from a local farmer, were grazing contentedly by the gate.

'They're all due to lamb in a couple of weeks', I said, 'and it will be a lovely experience for the children'.

I looked at our visitor and could see that she had a problem, but for the life of me I could not imagine what it could be. Finally, an apologetic look came over her face. 'I'm really sorry', she said, 'but I'm afraid we can't allow this. The risk is too great. Contagious abortion'.

'Contagious abortion?' I said in utter disbelief, 'but these are all young children'.

'I'm thinking of the adult staff', came her reply.

Short of throttling her I could see there was nothing further that I could do. Health and Safety had in its wisdom decreed that the harmless pleasure of seeing new-born lambs frolicking round their mothers would be denied to these children. I don't often get angry, but the thought did cross my mind that, if I was to continue walking round the reserve with this harridan any longer, it would put her health and safety at extreme risk. I therefore gave her a map and asked her to go wherever she wanted and then come back to the house and tell me if she found any other problems.

A pair of tawny owls on our reserve

If I had conceived for one moment that that would be the end of our worries I was in for a disappointment. 'You've got very many stinging nettles near the paths, and children and teachers could suffer severe stings' was her opening salvo.

'Take a deep breath' I said to myself, before patiently explaining the many advantages of nettles on a nature reserve, and then 'Anything else you're not happy about?' I said in a voice somewhat lacking in conviction.

'Yes, I'm afraid so. There are several dangerous areas – ponds, the river and a very steep bank. All of these require large warning notices. In capital letters', she added in case I had not heard her properly.

'Thank you', I said, 'very helpful'. Needless to say, apart from stopping lambing here, we took no further action. And we've had no further visits from Health and Safety. Like any responsible organization that looks after children we observe strict rules regarding child safety. There is, however, a world of difference between rules based on sound common-sense and some of the ridiculous restrictions that are part of the modern world. Climbing trees and taking part in conker fights used to be happy and harmless experiences.

That visit actually left me feeling very sad, particularly looking back to a time ten or so years previously. Then the teacher would have taken the class to the wood where they would have had their picnic lunches. After that it would be 'Boys to the right, girls to the left. Here's a spade and loo roll for each group, and make sure you don't leave any mess'.

Nowadays we have three separate loos – boys, girls and disabled – kindly installed by the Council. However, a new problem has, needless to say, now arisen. When children leave the classroom they go to various areas on the reserve, some of which are quite some distance away. 'Please, teacher, I want to go to the toilet' can no longer be resolved by a quick visit to a nearby bush or tree. Health and Safety has, in its wisdom, decreed that proper loos must now be used, but here, not surprisingly, there's another problem. No child can be allowed to walk back to the Centre unaccompanied. Far too many (unspecified) dangers apparently lurk en route. The whole class is therefore disrupted to enable a teacher or accompanying adult to take the child back to the Centre.

Fortuitously (and no thanks to Health and Safety) the problem has in fact now been resolved. Bunny, my wife, was recently invited to take part in Celebrity Mastermind. 'Over my dead body', was her understandable reaction. That, however, was before they told her that all contestants, irrespective of their scores, would be given several thousand pounds for their chosen charity.

Thanks to her the Daws Hall Trust is now the proud owner of an eco-loo in the centre of the reserve.

OVERLEAF *Prunus yedoensis pendula*

Roses Galore

There can hardly be a garden anywhere in the world that does not feature a rose. Thousands of different forms are now available, and every year rose growers launch new varieties on the market.

To trace their origins one needs to go back a very long time. On the basis of fossil evidence, it has now been established that they occurred in some form or other long before the advent of *Homo sapiens*. Garden cultivation of roses started at least five thousand years ago, almost certainly in China. One of the two oldest groups of garden roses grown today is the gallicas, and these were originally cultivated by the Greeks and the Romans. The other is the damasks, which came from the Middle East and moved down to Europe with the crusaders. The classification of 'old' rose is now accepted as one created before 1867, which embraces two other groups, the albas and the centifolias, the latter including the lovely moss roses.

My own love affair with old roses dates back to the 1970s when I paid a visit to the late Humphrey Brooke's garden at Claydon, near Ipswich. Seeing his wonderful collection, sprawling in a fairly informal fashion, and sensing the heady scent of many of these old cultivars and species, had a profound effect on me. I quickly found a special area in my own garden for Rosa Mundi, Fantin Latour, the moss rose William Lobb, and Charles de Mills. Others soon followed, and today we have approximately 150 different old roses.

←← Fantin Latour

← Rosa Mundi

For many years I have been somewhat sceptical of claims by rose growers that they have created modern forms with a scent comparable to that of the old roses, and have intentionally excluded them from the collection. One well-known rose grower, the late David Austin, has however persevered, and many of his more recent creations have indeed fulfilled this claim. Some of his best roses are now in this garden, and they certainly have the capacity of extending the flowering season of our roses.

As we also now own quite a large collection of trees, I have included a number of climbers and rambling roses. This does, I believe, give an added dimension to the garden, and some – notably Paul's Himalayan Musk, Rambling Rector and *Rosa banksiae* – have reached prodigious heights here.

If I was asked to list a dozen of my own favourite old roses these would include Fantin Latour (Centifolia, *c.* 1820), Charles de Mills (Gallica, *c.* 1800), Felicité Parmentier (Alba, 1830), Camaieux (Gallica, 1830), Belle sans Flatterie (Gallica, 1806), Blush Noisette (Noisette, *c.* 1780), *R. Gallica officinalis*, the Apothecary's Rose (Gallica, pre 1220), Cuisse de Nymphe (Alba, *c.* 1470), General Kleber (Moss, 1856), Madame Plantier (Alba, 1835), Mary Queen of Scots (Pimpinellifolia, v. old) Sombreuil (1850) and William III (Pimpinellifolia, *c.* 1820).

With Bunny and our Rambling Rector, which grows to fifty feet

↑↑ *R. Gallica officinalis*

↑ The Pilgrim

↑↑ Blush Noisette

↑ Grootendorst

↑↑ Ispahan   ↑↑ Graham Thomas

↑ Königin von Dänemark   ↑ Ville de Bruxelles

To me, gardening is an intensely personal experience. I do listen to Bunny, but thankfully our tastes are almost invariably the same, and I do listen to Melvyn, our loyal and long-suffering gardener, who has put up with my whims and foibles for the past twenty-five years. There are only three plants I really dislike and those are box, dahlias and rudbeckias. Thankfully, Bunny dislikes them even more than I do. She can't bear blue hydrangeas, which actually I find rather attractive, but here I am happy to bow to her wishes. (A word of apology is due here. There is, of course, nothing wrong with any of the plants on our hate list, all of which are loved by many. It is just a matter of personal taste). We both love blue in a garden, and one of my favourite plants is love-in-a-mist, or nigella. Every part of it makes the senses tingle – its feathery leaf, its delicate flower and then its plump seed-head all bring back memories of my childhood. We cram blue of all shades unashamedly into the garden.

Pale blue of course is the colour of mecanopsis, the Himalayan blue poppy, a plant that provides a real challenge for gardeners in East Anglia, where the soil and the growing conditions are far removed from those in Scotland. Mecanopsis actually grow surprisingly well here and, with a little help, have produced a stunning display every year, apart from 2018 when conditions were very similar to those in the Sahara. Preparing the soil is crucial, and this consists of digging in to an area of the garden which is slightly acid and slightly shady a mixture of well-rotted horse muck, old leaf mould and ericaceous

Nigella

Mecanopsis, or Himalayan blue poppy

compost. Mecanopsis seeds (usually from our own stock) are sown in the autumn, overwintered in a cool greenhouse and planted out in April or May. Regular watering with rainwater in the summer is essential. The same soil and growing conditions suit an equally stunning plant, the giant Himalayan lily *Cardiocrinum giganteum*, and we have been fortunate to succeed with these wonderful plants most years.

It is trees, however, that are my first love. For a tree to have survived the drift of continents, successive ice ages and the rise of mountain ranges is indeed remarkable. This, however, applies to *Ginkgo biloba*, the maidenhair tree, a conifer (curiously) which ranged worldwide in the days of the dinosaurs. Latterly, and for reasons unknown, it retreated to two small mountain areas in China. Nowadays, thankfully, it is a comparatively common plant in cultivation, and there are many lining the streets of London. These are almost invariably males and most people have never seen a female. Why? Because their fruit rots and gives off a terrible stench which has been likened by one authority to 'vegetable vomit'. In short, lady ginkgos, poor things, are short, fat and smelly.

The extraordinary resilience of the ginkgo not only enabled it to outlast the effects of two Ice Ages, but to be one of the very few living things to survive the atomic bombing of Hiroshima. Some trees, according to Chinese experts, are known to live for well over a thousand years. Recently, scientists have discovered that, by making use of pheromones, ginkgos have the ability of defending themselves against a variety of insect, bacterial and fungal adversaries.

Among other conifers that we grow here is one with an even more remarkable history. In fact it reads like a dendrological thriller – the discovery of a living fossil, a tree known

Knapweed and other wildflowers in their full glory

only from fossilized specimens and which was believed to have become extinct millions of years ago. The story of the rediscovery of this tree began in 1941 when a Japanese palaeobotanist was examining under his microscope some fossil specimens that had been sent to him by a colleague in America. He noticed that there was something curious about these fossils which were labelled taxodium (swamp cypress) and sequoia (coastal redwood). The leaf formations did not conform to either of these, and he accordingly published a paper in which he claimed to have found a new fossil genus which he named metasequoia.

In the same year, three thousand miles away, some Red Army soldiers were on the march, trying to evade Japanese troops that were in pursuit of them in eastern Sichuan. Planning to camp for the night in a small village called Mo-tao-chi, the Chinese commander sent one of their number ahead to ensure there was an adequate supply of firewood. By great good fortune this young man was a forester by training and he saw, on entering the village, a conifer that was unknown to him. He noticed that it was a deciduous species, so he asked the village schoolmaster to send him some leaf specimens in the spring. The leaves were sent – and lost. More specimens were sent – and these too were lost. Finally, in 1946, some more leaves were sent and these eventually landed on the desk of the head of the botanical institute in Beijing. This scientist, who had read the paper describing the new fossil genus, reached the startling conclusion that metasequoia was in fact alive and well three million years after it had died out in the rest of the world. He gave it a new scientific name, *Metasequoia glyptostroboides* and, after the war, specimens were collected and distributed to botanical gardens in various parts of the world. This new species grew and thrived in all sorts of soil and climatic conditions, and it is one of the descendants of the old conifer from Mo-tao-chi that now grows happily in this garden.

A growing number of other interesting or unusual trees and shrubs have now been added to the collection and, apart from our regular open days, we have started welcoming garden clubs and other interested groups for guided tours.

Magnolia Black Tulip

↖ *Magnolia soulangeana* Just Jean

← *Magnolia virginiana* Moonglow

↗ *Magnolia stellata* Water Lily

I have noticed over the years that many people are inclined to plant trees and then go away and forget about them. To me it is vital to look after them, first by giving them a good mulch for at least a couple of years, and longer if they look in need of it. Staking, to prevent wind-rock, is also important, as is shaping young trees. One third crown, two thirds stem is the general rule, and this should be done during the winter months when the sap is down. Here we are also particular about labelling our trees and shrubs. Not only does this help me remember complex Latin names, but it is certainly appreciated and commented on by many of our visitors. And do I talk to my trees? Yes, of course I do, and I honestly believe that a close association with one's plants is beneficial to both parties.

OVERLEAF *Clematis* Arabella with cornus in background

Buddleias, Butterflies and Bee-bums

One family of plants that has long interested me is the buddleias, of which we have around twenty different forms growing here. Like many other gardeners I love the many different varieties of the Butterfly bush *B. davidii* for the obvious reason that they attract butterflies and day flying moths. Thirty years ago, on a summer day, it was a common sight to see around thirty or more small tortoiseshells, red admirals and peacock butterflies on a single bush. Sadly, these numbers have been drastically reduced, partly due to climate change, but mainly because of our still uncontrolled use of insecticides. Now naturalised in many cities in the British Isles and commonly found on railway embankments, this species originated in China and Japan. Here we have several plants in the garden, and others have appeared naturally on the nature reserve, particularly in the wood where, thankfully, they seem to be immune from the mastications of muntjacs and rabbits. In the large glade that we have created, they attract speckled woods, and the occasional purple hairstreak and hummingbird hawk moth as well as the commoner species of butterflies.

One of the most attractive buddleias is *B. crispa*, from Afghanistan eastwards through the Himalayas into China. It is perfectly hardy in the West Country, but in East Anglia it is best taken into a greenhouse during the winter. Also growing to phenomenal heights in Cornwall is *B. colvilei,* which grows here to around ten foot (3 metres) on a sheltered south-facing wall.

Another excellent buddleia is *B. farreri*, (considered by some to be a variety of *B. crispa*) and named after the famous plant hunter Reginald Farrer. Perfectly hardy, *farreri* produces long panicles of rose pink flowers in April and May, after which it should be pruned. Another Chinese species which I can strongly recommend is *B. fallowiana*, both the nominate form and *f. alba*. Flowering later than *davidii*, both forms have very attractive white undersides to their leaves. Yet another excellent Chinese species is *B. officinalis* whose scent when it flowers in winter rivals that of any hyacinth or jasmine. This species can happily sit outside when the last frost is over, but needs bringing into a heated greenhouse or conservatory before it flowers. I must also mention *B. megalocephala*, a recent introduction from Guatemala. I first planted this species in a sheltered spot five years ago and it produced interesting small yellow flowers which turned to a burnt orange colour for the first time last year.

Finally, one of my most favourite buddleias, *B. salviifolia*, a semi-evergreen from South Africa with flowers that can either be white, mauve or purple. Grown in its native land the Xhosa people convert the wood into assegais, while a decoction of their roots is used to treat coughs or colic. Another winter flowerer with a superb scent and requiring a sheltered site, it benefits from hard pruning immediately after it has flowered.

In the wildflower meadow the dominant species for a number of years – see page 42 – was the ox-eye daisy, but gradually it decreased and after about five years it had virtually disappeared. This, I'm told, is not unusual. What was unusual was that several years later, without any warning, it started to appear, at least three hundred yards away, in the middle of the garden. There it has multiplied more and more each year – see frontispiece. Now, mown grass paths with hundreds of ox-eye daisies on either side add an interesting and attractive new dimension to the garden.

Nature has done this, but it got me thinking about what other wildflowers we could and should encourage in the garden. We have always used weedkillers as little as possible, but I have nevertheless waged a constant (losing) battle against brambles, stinging nettles, thistles, ground elder and bindweed. A number of other wildflowers have thrived and multiplied. In the spring we have cowslips, primroses, violets and bluebells, and a similar procession of other species continues throughout the growing season. Among these are purple loosestrife, hemp agrimony and meadowsweet, all of which thrive beside the streams and ponds that we have created.

 Triteleia uniflora

 Ox-eye daisies

Some of our
butterflies

← Small Copper

↙ Brown Argus

→ Comma

↓ Common Blue

↓↓ Gatekeeper

Another lover of damp areas is the Himalayan balsam or policeman's helmet, a non-native and invasive species, that was first introduced by gardeners in the 1930s. The spread of this plant accelerated dramatically in the 1950s and now it is present along most of the watercourses in southern England, particularly in the west country. We have it here along our stretch of the Stour, together with another invasive species, giant hemlock, and work parties go to the river annually to cut down both of these plants before they flower. Personally, I must admit to loving the aptly-named 'policeman's helmet' and allow it to grow in a secluded corner of the garden, far from water. There, on a summer's evening, I can watch bumblebees going head first into its massive flowers, which gives it yet another delightful local name – 'bee-bum'.

The occasional wild fritillary *Fritillaria meleagris* has appeared over the years in a number places, particularly one area in the garden with short dampish grass where I keep a small collection of *Cornus kousa* with its various forms. These (the *kousa*) do nothing until the summer when they produce a variety of coloured flowers, followed by strawberry-like fruit. This seemed an ideal area to try to establish a quantity of fritillaries, interspersed with the only native British tulip *Tulipa sylvestris*. This scheme worked very well, and we have now added several other forms of low-growing tulip species, together with primroses and wild wood anemones. The effect has been extremely rewarding.

The sanctuary is in fact the hub of the garden. It is where, a little over fifty years ago, I planted my first trees. It is also where, at the same time, I installed a borehole and excavated two parallel channels to take the water down to a large pond that had been created some time during the early part of the sixteenth century. That is when the builders of the day would have been looking for a source of clay for the daub and wattle required

Snakeshead fritillaries *Fritillaria meleagris*

Cornus kousa Satomi

Wild tulips *Tulipa sylvestris*

← *Cornus* Eddie's White Wonder

↓ *Cornus* Porlock

for the construction of the house. From this pond, following the natural contours of the land, we made two further ponds and laid land-drains between them to give a constant supply of fresh water.

Having plenty of water in the garden has proved to be a godsend. Nyssas (which the Americans call tupelos), cornus, taxodiums and gunneras thrive in these conditions, as do marginals such as pontaderias, primulas and dieramas which all give added colour and interest throughout the seasons.

Ideally, a garden should have something of interest throughout the year, and there is one tree, the amelanchier, which answers all those requirements. It has vivid new leaves, lovely white blossom, and excellent autumn colouring. Apart from that we have a mass of spring bulbs; roses and plenty more in the summer; eucryphias and cornus in August and September, and wonderful autumn colours throughout October and into early November. We are also fortunate in having two fine specimens of another tree, *Cercidiphyllum japonicum* (or katsura), that has a unique property in the autumn, which is to produce a curious but rather pleasant smell of burnt sugar. This is caused by a molecule called maltol, which is the same as the one released when sugar is burnt to make caramel.

→ Our gardener Melvyn Prentice with *Eucryphia nymansensis* Nymansay

OVERLEAF A carpet of snowdrops

↑ *Gunnera manicata* from South America

→ *Betula albosinensis septentrionalis* from China

January and February are dismissed by many people as being of little or no interest in the garden, but with careful planning there are many plants that are actually seen at their best at this time of year. Three unrelated 'h's' come to mind – heathers, hellebores and hamamelis (or witch hazel). Holly berries are lovely, but so also are the berries of skimmia, callicarpa, malus, sorbus and many others. Then there is the bark or stems of a number of trees and shrubs, which are particularly beautiful in the winter. Here we have *Prunus serrula*, several white-barked birches and a lot of dogwoods, of which *Cornus alba sibirica* and Mid-winter Fire are very effective at this time of year. *Acer palmatum* Sangokaku is probably my favourite, with its scarlet stems, and it is unbelievably beautiful when snow is on the ground.

We only had a few aconites in the sanctuary, but our kind neighbour, Rob, had masses under his trees, and he said to Jonathan 'help yourself'. This Jonathan did with a vengeance, and then he turned his hand to our snowdrops. Quite large groups were virtually hidden under bushes on the reserve, and these he dug up and divided into much smaller clumps which he then replanted in the garden. Having done what he wanted to do there, he then proceeded to carry out a similar operation on the reserve. Anyway, so successful has he been that we now host Snowdrop Open Days in February which raise extra funds for the Trust.

By and large I try and stick to the law during my various gardening activities, but I must admit that many years ago there was one notable exception. It occurred when I was the proud possessor of a large collection of exotic pheasants, many of which were endangered in the wild. At that time there was only one of the fifty-odd species of pheasant that had never been successfully kept or bred in captivity anywhere in the world. This was the Blood Pheasant, a little-known denizen of the high altitudes in Nepal, China and Tibet. The story of my trapping and bringing my original pair of these birds to England has been told in my book, *Blood Pheasant, a Himalayan Adventure* (Mitre Press), 1971.

It was while I was in Nepal that I discovered that marijuana (or hashish) was readily available and, not surprisingly, I succumbed to the temptation. Not only did I thoroughly enjoy the experience, but I brought a few seeds of *Cannabis sativa* back to England and planted them in a remote corner of the vegetable garden. Six plants flourished and were almost ready for harvesting when the telephone rang. It was Tom, the village policeman.

'Morning, Major, how are we?'

'Fine, Tom, what can I do for you?'

'Sorry, Major, but I need to see you urgent like. Can I come up right away?'

Panic ensued. Oh, God! Someone had told the police. I quickly grabbed a spade, raced down to the vegetable garden, dug up my precious plants and promptly buried them. I just got back to the house as Tom's police car drove in.

'Sorry about the rush, Major, but I've just seen that your shotgun licence expired last week, and I'll be in real trouble if I don't renew it for you PDQ.'

So ended the little saga of my illicit importation and, worse still, any ideas of a happy puff or two on my home-grown cannabis.

→ *Acer japonicum laciniatum* in the autumn

OVERLEAF View of the island pond in Summer

All Creatures Great and Small

And what of the various mammals, birds and other creatures that share our lives here?

Badgers, generally speaking, have a bad press among farmers, due to the fact that they are proven carriers of bovine tuberculosis, but they are also much loved by naturalists. The late Lord Arran, whose wife was a cousin of mine by marriage, was responsible, despite being only spasmodic in his attendance at the House of Lords, for two important pieces of legislation. The first of these was the 1967 Sexual Offences Act that liberalised homosexuality, while the second was the 1973 Badgers Act that gave Mr. Brock legal protection. Arran used to delight in telling his friends that one of these prevented people from badgering buggers, while the other stopped people buggering badgers.

Prior to 1908 badgers had few friends. Badger baiting and badger digging were commonplace activities, and gamekeepers trapped or shot any creature that they considered a threat to their precious gamebirds. That year, however, saw the publication of 'Wind in the Willows' by my namesake, Kenneth Grahame, and since then children of all ages have delighted in the adventures of Mole, Ratty, Toad and Badger, the last named of which became the emblem of the county wildlife trusts. When I was a child the only badger I ever saw was one that had been trapped by Cecil, my gamekeeper friend, and certainly in our part of East Anglia they were not common at all.

Legal protection cannot in itself explain the phenomenal population explosion of these animals that has occurred in many parts of Britain, especially in the last twenty or thirty years. One reason, however, must surely be that a species multiplies or decreases in direct correlation to its food supply. Apart from the huge increase of chemical fertilizers, pig-, cow-, and horse-muck have never before been so liberally applied to the land, be it farm or garden. This has brought with it a massive increase in the earthworm population, of which a single badger can consume over two hundred in a night.

Personally, I must confess to having a love-hate relationship with these creatures, of which we probably have around twenty or thirty on the nature reserve. Many people, young and old, have enjoyed magical summer evenings, sitting quietly with me and watching the delightful antics of our badgers and their cubs. When, as is often the case, I go up there on my own, the cubs are even more confident. One night I nearly lost my shoe. I had put a dollop of honey on it and one cub wasn't content to just lick it off! On occasions when they dig up the lawn, however, my language becomes unprintable, and I can certainly sympathise with farmers and their antipathy towards these animals.

Apart from badgers we have a good selection of mammals on the reserve. Longworth traps are put out overnight by the teachers, to enable children to see and learn about

Badger cubs

voles, wood mice, yellow-necked mice, or the occasional shrew which are caught and subsequently released. Footprints (or tracks) of a variety of mammals – foxes, badgers, otters, rabbits and others – can be seen throughout the reserve, and children learn to identify these. Alas, we have no hedgehogs and, sadly, we are unlikely to have them so long as we have badgers.

We have two species of deer – the roe (with their prominent white hindquarters) and the muntjac – the latter, which are half the size of the roe, are the oldest known deer, having first appeared as long as twenty million years ago, with remains found in Miocene deposits in France, Germany and Poland. Their true habitat now is many parts of southern Asia, but feral populations began to appear in this country in the nineteen twenties. These were predominantly escapees from Woburn Abbey, where the then Duke of Bedford kept a large collection of exotic deer. Unlike other deer, they have no seasonal rut, can breed at any time of the year, and are rapidly on their way to becoming the most numerous deer species in Britain. They are responsible for the destruction of much of the under-storey in our wood, which is one reason for the decline of the nightingale and many of our warblers. Thankfully, most of our garden is in a fenced area, but without this protection I dread to think what damage the muntjac would cause, particularly to our collection of old roses.

When I came here, I was able to sit quietly by the river or the Losh-house Brook and watch Ratty and his water vole friends and family plopping into the water or grooming their whiskers. Gradually they appeared to decline in numbers and by the mid nineteen-nineties they had totally disappeared from here. The culprit was a non-native invader, the mink. Introduced from North America for fur farming in the twenties, a number

Jonathan Clarke and mink

of mink escaped and began to breed in the wild. Then, to add to the problem, animal rights activists raided mink farms in the nineties and released many more. Inevitably, the consequences for our native fauna, plus chicken farms, game farms and others was disastrous. I began to set traps for mink on the reserve and succeeded in killing half a dozen or so. What depressed me then was the attitude of the local county wildlife trust. Robbie, my friend who had been so helpful in setting up our nature reserve, had sadly died and these were new people whose attitudes seemed to be that every living creature, native or non-native, should be preserved. I was not prepared to do this and our trustees unanimously agreed that, sadly, we should sever our links with this organization. With help from the Game Conservancy and like-minded landowners along the River Stour and the neighbouring River Colne we organized a team of trappers. Gradually the tide started to turn and water voles, the most endangered mammal in the country, began, very slowly, to make a comeback here and in other parts of the country.

Ignorance, in my opinion, is responsible for many of the ill-founded attitudes of so many people, not only towards the mink, but also towards the grey squirrel, which is another non-native species, having also been introduced from North America at the end of the nineteenth century. Grey squirrels are mainly responsible for the wholesale decline of our native red squirrels by spreading a form of pox to which they themselves are immune, but which is fatal to the red. They steal birds' eggs, eat young birds and cause incalculable damage to trees.

Woodland is an important habitat on the reserve, and looking under logs and leaf litter is a fascinating and instructive activity for children. It is there that a whole new world is opened up to them. Woodlice, spiders, worms, stag beetles and other strange-looking creatures lurk there. They may even find a slow-worm, which is in fact neither slow, nor a worm, nor indeed a snake, but a legless lizard. These delightful reptiles usually measure up to eighteen inches in length and they prey on worms, slugs and a variety of insects. When autumn comes groups numbering up to thirty retire into deep burrows where they hibernate. In the spring they come out, mate, and in August or September the young slow-worms, measuring one to two inches, hatch on emergence. The only true snake we have here is the grass snake, a perfectly harmless creature, usually measuring three to four foot, which we see regularly close to water or sometimes even swimming. It is easily identified by the yellowish-white 'collar' round its neck, and it feeds on frogs, newts, small fish and mice. The females lay their eggs, numbering ten to forty, in our compost heaps where the heat is sufficient to incubate them.

Kingfishers are regularly seen along the river or stream, as are grey wagtails (which many people wrongly call yellow wagtails), and countless reed warblers can be seen and heard in the spring. Garden birds are reasonably plentiful here, including both forms of thrush, goldfinches, tits, nuthatches and many others. The annual migration brings house martins, which nest at the front of the house, swallows and various warblers. Cuckoos and spotted flycatchers, two species that are declining nationally, are among

Slow-worm   Spotted Flycatcher

Turtle Doves

our regular summer visitors, and not a year has gone by when I have not heard the telephone-ringing call of the male turtle dove. In 2017, Bunny photographed a pair of these nationally endangered birds on our bird-table, only to get an exactly similar photograph in 2018. Presumably the same pair returning?

House martins usually arrive here around the middle of April. Little do these inter-continental travellers realise what joy and relief they bring. Every morning, from the beginning of that month, when the curtains have been drawn and we are sitting in bed with our early morning tea, Bunny and I scan the southern sky waiting for the miracle to appear. Dreadful thoughts cross our minds. Have they failed to cross the Sahara? Have they fallen to some trigger-happy Algerian or Frenchman? Then, at last, the sight we've been waiting for – at first only a few, on a reconnaissance it would seem, flying up to make sure the remains of last year's nests are still there. Then, a week or so later, the main body arrives, wings whirring as they pass within inches of each other as we watch another of nature's miracles – never a mid-air collision – as the serious business of repair work and rebuilding is carried out. Nearby is a permanent source of damp mud and also, in the air all around them, no shortage of insect food. By the middle of May, after an incubation period of just two weeks, young chicks will have hatched and three weeks after that many will have already taken to the wing. Still the incessant workload continues and man, if there is any humility in him, can only look on in wonder.

Normally, each pair has two broods and, in a good year, three. Then, all too soon, the time has come for them to head south, usually leaving just one or two nests where the young have not fully fledged. The main party is suddenly no longer with us. That, however, is not the end. Amazingly, they have one final surprise in store for us. A week or so after we have prematurely bid them *bon voyage*, without any warning, the sky is suddenly full of them once more. We watch with fascination, from the comfort of our bed, and wonder what the purpose of this final visit is. Martin after martin flies up to a nest, a brief touch (or maybe not even that), and it's back into the sky for another circuit. Are these birds memorizing exactly where, in around eight months' time, and after a return journey of many thousands of miles, and after countless hazards, they must somehow endeavour to return? Or, are these purely social, 'getting-to-know you' visits in preparation for their long migratory journey to Africa? I remember standing in the Pyrenees, one year at the end of September, looking up and seeing wave after wave of swallows and house martins, in packs of several hundred, flying southwards.

Red-breasted geese and young

↑ *Acer palmatum* Osakazuki

← *Acer triflorum* in the autumn

A good friend of ours, a bird ringer from Yorkshire who has spent many years studying these birds, tells me that not only are adult birds known to move colonies mid-season, but that wife swapping or husband swapping can occur between broods. Clearly, there is still much that we do not know about these delightful birds, with their somewhat questionable moral standards.

Being a keen amateur ornithologist enables me to watch and to appreciate the varying bird life that we have here according to the changing seasons. For more than fifty years I have kept a large diary in which I have recorded, not only sightings of particular interest, but also the arrival dates of our regular spring migrants. For example, the earliest recording of a chiffchaff was 10th March 1989, and the earliest cuckoo was 29th March 1984.

Nature reserves can and generally do record unusual sightings and here we can claim the following: bittern, hoopoe, long-tailed duck, black kite, greenshank, crossbill and a small party of black terns. One of the most unusual records here was of a sociable plover, a bird that should by rights have been in an area to the north of the Caspian Sea. This was very shortly after we had come to Daws Hall and, in my naivety I thought it was only helpful to put a notice in the local newspaper. Twenty-four hours later the local lanes were jammed with twitchers from as far afield as Exeter and the Isle of Man. Sadly, by then the bird had flown.

Several years later I was wandering along our stretch of the Stour when up jumped a purple heron, a bird that I knew well from my time in East Africa. This part of the river Stour is in fact the boundary between Suffolk and Essex, so I duly reported the sighting to the wildlife trusts of both counties. Back came identical queries: 'which county was it in?' I thought long and hard before replying that it was standing in the middle of the river with its legs apart.

Yes, we have had unusual sightings, and undoubtedly there will be more. For example, in 2017 a pair of ravens nested at a site in Essex only ten miles from here, the first breeding record in Essex since 1890. The following year they nested again, a mere stone's throw from here, and young and old were regularly seen and heard on this reserve and in the garden.

Sadly, however, the general pattern of bird life both here and elsewhere in the country is on a downward trend. Many species are holding their own, a few are increasing, but the status of others is far from healthy. During the 1970s and 1980s corncrakes, corn buntings and nightjars were still nesting not far from here. Now there are none. On this reserve, tree sparrows and migratory yellow wagtails were relatively common. Again, now there are none. My diary tells me that in 1984, and again in 1988, over two hundred snipe and more than three hundred golden plover were regularly wintering on the meadow adjoining this reserve. Now, if we see a handful of each we are lucky. Two species that do still regularly breed here are turtle doves and spotted flycatchers.

Someone who has given us invaluable help for more than thirty years is Peter, who is a bird ringer licensed by the British Trust for Ornithology. Detailed records have been kept by him since he started ringing here in 1985. During that period he has ringed here close on four thousand birds of fifty-three different species.

During the summer literally hundreds of banded demoiselles congregate along the river, and other members of the *libellulinae* (dragonflies and damsel flies), of which close on twenty different species have been recorded here, may be seen wherever we have water. Autumn brings out the largest members of the family, the hawkers, some of which are almost the size of a small bird. All of this group spend the early stages of their lives as nymphs, or naiads, in the water.

To most people moths are boring brown creatures that fly at night and make holes in our jumpers. In fact there are around two and a half thousand different moths in Britain and many of these are wonderfully coloured. One third are known as macrolepidoptera (or 'macros'), and it is only these that are studied by most people. The remaining 'micros' are often minute and, because of their very small size, are extremely hard to tell apart. We have run moth traps here for many years, partly to be able to show visiting children

← Eider drake, one of the pinioned species of waterfowl that we keep

some of the larger and more interesting species, but also, with the help of local experts, to be able to record a comprehensive list of the moths on this reserve. To date they number in excess of seven hundred.

Some of these moths, like the lappet and the buff-tip, are masters of camouflage, while others sport wonderfully varied colour patterns and are considerably larger than our

↖↖ Peter Dwyer and the first nightingale breeding record, Daws Hall, May 2013

↖ A young nightingale

← Banded demoiselle ♂

↗↗ Buff-tip

↗ Black Arches

→ Emperor

Elephant Hawk-moth

Unusual colour form of Poplar Hawk-moth

butterflies. I well remember an occasion when Bunny's two grandsons, Frederic and Benedict, were with us and we ran our moth trap. Both boys were familiar with many of the species, and that night there was light cloud-cover and we had a very successful catch. (Strange as it may seem, if there is a full moon, many moths head off in that direction rather than to an electric light bulb). Anyway, that night we caught several different hawk-moths and an emperor, and the two boys had great fun lifting some of

Amy Sutcliffe with
two young pupils

these gently and placing them on their jerseys. I went over to the Centre where a small class of A-level students from a local secondary school were just finishing their lunch break.

'Would you like to see some of the moths we caught last night?' I asked.

At that moment Frederic and Benedict came in to the Centre where there was a mixed reaction. One seventeen-year-old boy ran screaming out of the door; another asked if he could hold the emperor moth, but only if we could guarantee it wouldn't bite him. The remaining children were clearly fascinated by creatures they had never seen before and wanted to know more about them.

'We're running a moth course in a couple of weeks' time', Amy, our teacher, said. Suffice it to say that five boys immediately signed up. Hopefully, this was the start of a new and fascinating interest for them.

OVERLEAF The bottom pond with *Cornus contraversa variegata* in the centre

We Must Not Give Up

Neither I nor any of our loyal and helpful trustees will forget the year 2010. I knew something was up around October because of the increased number of visits to our schoolroom by representatives of Essex County Council. This, it will be remembered, was the organization that, twenty-five years previously, had entered into a legal agreement, not only to give us an annual grant equating to the salary of a groundsman, but also to appoint and fund our environmental teacher.

Essex, together with other counties, it must be admitted, had recently suffered massive cuts to its budget and was being forced to make savings. I was, however, sad and not a little angry that there were no prior discussions with me whatsoever, and all I received was an abrupt letter informing me that as from 1 April 2011 all support from the Council would cease. To do this to the one environmental education centre that gave maximum inspiration to the young of Essex was surely a short-sighted decision.

I talked through the implications of this sudden bombshell with Simon, who had by then been with us for over twenty years and had become something of a legend. People who had been taught by him were bringing their children here, hoping that the man who had taught them so much when they themselves were young would still be here. His reaction to the news was identical to mine. If we were to call a halt to this successful operation, there would, quite rightly, be an outcry from all the schools that regularly came here. Our environmental teaching and our facilities were, by then, second to none. He then informed me that he had just been offered early retirement by the Council, but if we were somehow to carry on, he would be happy to continue working here on a self-employed basis for the next four years, after which he planned to retire. We then had a meeting of our trustees, and the unanimous decision was not to throw in the towel, but somehow to battle on. The crucial factor of course was funding. Between us we managed, fortunately, to get quite a lot of extra money, both from grant-giving trusts and from kind friends. There is no doubt that our good track record over the past twenty-five years was a factor in our favour. Our financial shortfall continues, however, and that is why I am happy to donate part of any revenue that I get from the sale of this book to the Daws Hall Trust. Essex did kindly relent somewhat and, from 2013 to 2018, they gave us a small grant, but now we get nothing at all from either Suffolk or Essex County Councils.

← *Nyssa sylvatica*, with *Salvia uliginosa* in the foreground and a *Liquidambar* Lane Roberts in the background

OVERLEAF Some wild and garden plants in a naturalized state

Beekeeping

I mentioned earlier my love of bees and my involvement with beekeeping as a boy. I never had the opportunity to keep bees while I was a soldier, but once we had settled into life at Daws Hall I was determined to start again. Somebody mentioned to me that beginners' courses were being held at the local agricultural college, so I promptly enrolled at one taking place the following month. I duly arrived on the appointed day to find six other would-be beekeepers, all dressed as though they were going to outer space. The instructor, who was similarly attired, gave an enquiring glance in my direction.

'Sorry if I'm late', I said. 'I've come to join the beekeeping class'.

The enquiring look changed to one of total amazement. 'I'm afraid you can't join the course unless you've got proper protective clothing', he said. 'You know, veil, bee-suit, boots and gloves', he added, and I saw the other students looking at me as though I was mad.

I did purchase a veil, as I didn't want to get stung in the mouth or eye, and I did buy a beginner's guide to beekeeping, which taught me a lot. Apart from that I found to my surprise that a lot of the simple skills which I had learnt as a boy came back to me. A kind local beekeeper took me under his wing, and I gradually got to the stage where I had half a dozen beehives and, with the help of Jonathan, we were producing a good crop of honey. I never went on the course, nor did I ever dress for a journey to outer space.

We desperately wanted children to have the opportunity to learn about these wonderful creatures. The next stage was therefore to convert an unused shed on the sanctuary to a 'bee room'. With the help of a local beekeeper, an observation hive was installed, together with instructive wall charts, so that children and their teachers could, in total safety, learn about the intricate life of the honeybee. They were also able to tell the difference between the queen, who had a coloured mark on her thorax, the drones (or males) and the workers. They could also watch the 'waggle dance' of the bees and, with the help of one of the charts, learn what this meant. They could see too the queen moving from cell to cell to deposit her eggs, and the worker bees bringing in nectar from our wildflowers and garden plants and depositing it in one of the 'supers'. This venture proved to be very popular, not just with the children, but with teachers, visiting parents and grandparents, and the general public on open days.

Whenever we had honey to spare we put a number of pots in the bee room, for sale to the public. On one occasion we had had a bumper crop and Jean, a good friend in the

Hiving a swarm

village, offered to sit in the bee room and act as cashier during the afternoon. The day went well, the sun shone, plenty of visitors came and all the honey was sold. Jean told me at the end of the afternoon that one woman had come in to the bee room, shortly after we had opened, and said that she had been sent by her family to buy forty pots. 'You've got the best honey in East Anglia', she announced triumphantly as she handed over the money and shovelled forty pots in to two large carrier bags, 'I wasn't too sure whether to allow her to take such a large amount', Jean said, 'but she was a pretty formidable woman, and clearly not one to argue with'. I thanked Jean very much for her help and hoped that that was the end of the story. It wasn't.

The following day the telephone rang. 'I bought a lot of honey from you yesterday' came a haughty voice at the other end of the line. 'We are not at all happy with it. I'll return it to you this afternoon and I want my money back'.

'Oh, what's wrong with it?' I asked as politely as I could.

'It's not as good as the honey we had last year. It tastes quite different'.

If it had been rape honey I could have seen that she had a point, but it wasn't. I explained as patiently as I could that bees go to different sources of nectar at different times of the year, frequently resulting in slightly different tastes. Her honey, I told her, came mainly from our wildflower meadow, plus various garden sources like lavender, gaura and lime. Finally, I told her that I was very sorry but I was not prepared to refund her, adding that all the money that was made on our honey went not to me but to our Trust, which was a registered charity.

'You'll hear more of this', she announced before the line went dead.

Months went by and I had almost forgotten about the incident. Again it was the telephone, but this time a different voice. 'Trading Standards', the caller announced. 'We've had a complaint about you which we need to investigate'.

'And what have I done wrong?' I enquired in as patient a voice as I could muster.

'It's your honey' came the reply. 'I need to come and collect a pot to send off for analysis. We have reason to believe that it may not be pure honey'.

I took a deep breath. We really were beginning to get into the realms of fantasy. Anyway, the young lady arrived the next day and I duly handed over a pot of our honey.

'Just before you go' I said, 'would you mind telling me who in Chelmsford is going to analyze my honey?'

'Oh, it's not going to be analysed in this country' she said.

By now I was not just mystified but speechless.

'It'll be sent to Brussels', she explained.

Months went by; spring emerged as did my bees: a new honey season had begun. Eventually the lady from Trading Standards rang me once more.

'We've had the result through', she said 'and it showed conclusively that what was in your pot was indeed pure honey'.

I was just about to comment, fairly tersely, that I could have told her that in the first place, and what a bloody waste of time and money, when she continued: 'I'm afraid, however, that you have committed an offence under EU law. I will explain this to you when I come and see you'.

She arranged to come to the house later that day and I was left wondering whether I was going to be dragged off to Brussels in handcuffs. When she did come she had in her hand the label from my offending pot of honey. 'You see that', she said, pointing to the bottom of the label where, quite correctly I thought, was printed   **1lb** 454gm

'What's the matter with that?' I asked. I simply could not see what could possibly be wrong with these labels, which had been printed for me by a firm that supplied all manner of bee equipment – hives, smokers, protective clothing, honey jars, labels and so on – to professional and amateur beekeepers up and down the length and breadth of the country. The only thing that they had added when I ordered these labels was our name and address.

'Under EU law', came her condescending reply, '454 grams has to precede one pound and be in bolder type-setting.

This little incident necessitated the calling in and reprinting of thousands of honey jar labels nationwide … and no guesses as to how I voted in the recent Referendum.

Never too young to learn

WORKER   QUEEN   DRONE

Worker, queen and drone bees

OVERLEAF Autumn on the island pond. *Photograph by Nicola Stocken*

Back to School

The animal kingdom is so vast and so varied that, even in this tiny corner of East Anglia where I have been fortunate enough to have lived for over fifty years, I know only a tiny fraction of the other creatures that are on this reserve. For example no mention has been made of the molluscs, the ladybirds, the flies, the bumblebees, the spiders, or indeed the coleoptera (or beetles), which form the largest order of insects with well over a quarter of a million known species.

All the teachers who have worked here, however, have contacts in these various disciplines. This has not only enabled us to run courses on wildflowers, bats, birdsong, fungi, moths and so on, but to help maintain up-to-date lists of some of the lesser known families. For example, a recent bryophyte survey conducted here by specialists recorded six species of liverworts and no less than forty-seven mosses. Likewise, a mollusc survey found approximately forty different species of slugs, snails and mussels. All relevant information is passed on to county and national recorders, and this in turn helps us all to prepare management plans for the better understanding and conservation of these species.

Common spotted orchids

In this eight-acre garden we have now managed to assemble a fairly large collection of rare and unusual trees and shrubs from around the world, almost all of which are labelled. Conducted tours are arranged and the response from garden clubs, Women's Institute members, photographic societies and others has been very heartening. The same applies to the plant kingdom, where I have only touched on a few of the wildflowers that we have here. Only recently one species of wildflower has appeared which has always been scarce in Suffolk and Essex and which is now extinct in many of its old sites. This is betony, or *Stachys officinalis*.

Watching some of the numerous visits here by groups of schoolchildren gives me an opportunity to cast my mind back to my own childhood and to my time at school. Not surprisingly I can see huge differences in the then and now. Discipline in virtually all levels of society was certainly much stricter then, as was the influence of parents, teachers and religion. Certainly in Scotland, where my forebears came from, the Sabbath as a day of rest was strictly observed, and I can remember many of the older folk devoting much of the day to reading the bible. When I was young, we did have a few bullies, but I don't remember any rebels among us. At school we all tried our best and, in varying degrees, achieved passable results. Those who found the work difficult were, I'm ashamed to say, described as 'thick' and often punished, not infrequently with the cane, for their shortcomings. Now they are classed as dyslexic and, quite rightly, treated very differently. (Interestingly, that word only appears in the addenda section of my 1973 issue of the OED).

Today Daws Hall delivers education sessions to a wide variety of groups, and each one receives a carefully planned and tailored experience. Although the activities are aligned to the National Curriculum and further education specifications, Amy, our excellent teacher, always strives to offer so much more. Sensitive management of the reserve over the past forty years has created a wide variety of habitats within a relatively small area, making it an ideal setting both for teaching and for learning.

Pupils have the opportunity to be immersed in nature – often a novel experience for them – and to see creatures that, not infrequently, they never knew existed. Sometimes, particularly with older students, this is at first met with a streak of disinterestedness, or occasionally worse. However, after a brief display of histrionics at the sight of a harvestman or grasshopper, a sudden change occurs. The innate fascination that we all share for other living things slowly unfurls.

'This transition', Amy recently told me, 'never ceases to impress me. A boy or girl, who was at first determined that they would not, or could not, venture into the long vegetation, gradually wades further and further into the wildflower meadow. Then, clearly fascinated by what they see, they will squat or kneel and start to record the plants and insects that are around them. Often they will comment on the variety of different

In the flower meadow

organisms they see, having found a new appreciation for the beauty and complexity of nature. This is particularly evident when we use the moth trap, to show people of all ages the numerous but rarely encountered species whose beauty and variety always amazes them.'

'Working with primary schoolchildren is always a joy', she says. 'We usually start the day by opening Longworth mammal traps that have been set the night before, so that they can view and release the furry creatures inside. Quite often this is the first time these children will have seen a wild mouse or shrew. Some are wary, expecting to see something unpleasant, but after a few minutes studying the beady eyes and twitching whiskers of a wood mouse or bank vole, they are totally hooked. One of the most common questions is 'can we hold it?'.'

When I watch children splashing in the stream, as they try to find invertebrates that live and hide among the stones, or see their expressions of glee as they discover an eft lurking beneath a log, it is really rewarding. So too are the looks of concentration as they pick and try to identify leaves from different trees in the wood. We always hope that they will remember these days fondly and that some of the joy of being out in the natural world stays with them throughout their lives. Planting this seed of appreciation of nature is perhaps the most important thing that we aim to do.

Most groups only get the opportunity to visit once a year on a school trip, but we also work with Home Educators, who have made Daws Hall an important part of their

On the dipping platform

learning experience. For this, Amy has put together a unique programme that spans a whole year, taking in all of the seasonal changes and opportunities that these present. It is wonderful to see these families becoming increasingly familiar with the reserve and adding to their knowledge on every visit.

Our tuition is not limited to younger people and we are always happy to put together special programmes for adult and disabled groups. Amateur artists and photographic clubs come here and take advantage of the changing scenery and vibrant colours. Families are welcome during the school holidays to explore the reserve on Wild and Crafty days. Each month Holly, a popular and enthusiastic Forest School instructor, runs a special morning for pre-school children, who are accompanied by a parent or grandparent. These Out and Abouter events are immensely popular, as are her Forest School sessions. This movement, which started in Scandinavia in the 1950s, encourages child-led learning in all weathers throughout the year, in which children use a variety of tools and learn to manage appropriate risks. A proper appreciation of nature is central to all this tuition.

The following are just some of the numerous appreciative messages sent to our teaching staff:

'I have been bringing A level students to Daws Hall for the past ten years. It is an ideal site for Biology and Environmental Studies at all levels. The nature reserve

In the classroom

What has the bird ringer caught today?

In the bird hide

provides a range of stunning habitats that would be difficult to match in such a compact area. The students that I have brought here over the years always recall their visit to Daws Hall as one of the highlights of their school year.' L. R., St. Albans Catholic High School

'I am in awe of how much you pack in and how interesting and fun you make it. I can honestly say nothing we have ever done like this has ever come close to the fabulous learning opportunities you provide, so thank you very much.' S. M., Suffolk Home Educators Group.

'Dear Amy, thank you for making my day so special. It was the best day ever! You've helped me understand how much nature should mean to everyone!' Lula, Year 4, St. Margaret's Prep School.

'Wonderful nature reserve with a variety of habitats to explore. Amy was really helpful and knowledgeable as our guide.' Photographic Club.

'A truly beautiful place to visit. We had a wonderful afternoon on your last Open Day, exploring with our 2 year old daughter, just right for children as it's a lovely adventure with lots of trails. The pond dipping was great fun too and the cream tea to finish off was perfect. A great place to visit for all with something for everyone and a friendly/knowledgeable team to boot. We certainly aim to return!' A. B.

Final Thoughts

School visits here enable children of all ages to study various aspects of the national curriculum in what we believe to be the excellent environment that has been created over the past fifty years. In a nutshell, we give children a wonderful area for studying for their various exams, but can we offer them more? Do their visits here bring them any closer to nature? I hope the answer is an emphatic 'yes'.

Nowadays the sheer pace of life and the seemingly endless need for people to check on their mobiles tend to take young and old further and further away from the natural world. When I was young, my mentor and closest companion was Cecil, the gamekeeper at my old home. Instinctively I learned to copy his ways, to know the songs of the birds, the tracks in the woods, and the varying moods of hornets and honeybees. I was able to walk through a wood silently, without cracking a twig, to make crude bows and arrows out of hazel and elder, and to winkle a trout out of a stream and to flick it on to the bank. Advancing years have now dimmed many of these senses and skills, but wherever I go my eyes and ears still notice things that others miss. Many years ago I was lucky enough to visit the Taj Mahal, the famous mausoleum created by the Mogul emperor, Shah Jahan, for his beloved wife Mumtaz Mahal, close on four hundred years ago. Gazing at it in awe from where I stood in the Persian water garden that represented Paradise, I remember wondering whether any of the thousands of other visitors that day had spotted the swarm of bees that was clustered just beneath the onion-shaped dome. I offered a silent prayer of gratitude for a twofold experience that will remain with me till my dying day.

When I was young it was only natural (and sometimes compulsory) to go to church and I usually came away feeling refreshed and strengthened in spirit. Nowadays, as we all know, for the most part it is predominantly the old people who attend. The inescapable fact is we are destroying our natural world and ignoring God at an alarming rate.

Several years ago, when I was regularly putting out food for our badgers, I was approached by a good friend who was running that excellent charity, Success after Stroke. One of their patients, an elderly man who was fairly disabled, had never seen a badger in his life and desperately wanted to see one. Could I possibly help? I promised to do my best. The appointed evening came and, with a little help, I got him into my car and succeeded in driving to within about a hundred yards of the sett. He was so excited that he kept on talking in a loud voice, so I had to explain that if there was any noise at all the badgers would stay underground. Holding my hand and walking with great difficulty we inched our way quietly towards the sett. On part of the path in front of us and about twenty yards short of the viewing point there were quite a lot of dead sticks. I had negotiated these on my own countless times without making a noise, but how would it go with a disabled man clinging to me? Inevitably, he stumbled through this part of the path, far from silently. Then, when we were finally clear of this obstacle, I got him to sit on a nearby bench. Holding my breath I crept forward on my own. Mercifully, two adult badgers were quietly feeding on the peanuts that I had put out for them. I had placed two chairs overlooking the setts, so now all that remained was to negotiate the last few yards with him. All went well and we managed to watch the two badgers, plus a half-grown cub that came out to join them, for a good ten minutes. That was when he got a coughing fit, but it could not have mattered less. He had seen his first badger and he was a happy man.

Nature, in all its infinite beauty and mystery, has so much to offer us, and the earlier in life that young people can grasp this, the better it is, both for their pleasure and for their soul. It doesn't matter whether it is picking up discarded feathers or eggshells, making daisy chains, hunting for mushrooms, or sitting quietly in a wood listening to the song of the birds. Nature is there, waiting to be discovered, waiting to be enjoyed.

On the walkway over the scrape   One small happy child

List of Trees and Shrubs at Daws Hall

> * Essex Champion Tree
> ** English Champion Tree
> *** British Champion Tree
>   as awarded by The Tree Register

Abelia grandiflora
Abeliophyllum distichum
* *Abies grandis*
Abies pinsapo
Acacia baileyana purpurea
Acacia pravissima
* *Acer cappadocicum aureum*
* *Acer cissifolium*
Acer conspicuum Phoenix
Acer × conspicuum Silver Vein
Acer crataegifolium veitchii
Acer davidii Rosalie
Acer davidii Serpentine
Acer freemanii Autumn Blaze
Acer griseum
* *Acer henryi*
Acer japonicum aconitifolium
Acer japonicum laciniatum
Acer japonicum vitifolium
Acer micranthum
Acer maximowiczianum
Acer negundo aureomarginatum
Acer palmatum Beni Zuru
Acer palmatum Bloodgood
Acer palmatum Butterfly
Acer palmatum corallinum
Acer palmatum dissectum
Acer palmatum dissectum Emerald Lace
Acer palmatum Ellen
Acer palmatum Fujinami Nishiki
Acer palmatum heptalobum
Acer palmatum Katsura
Acer palmatum linearilobum
Acer palmatum Osakazuki
Acer palmatum Sango-kaku
Acer palmatum Villa Taranto
* *Acer pectinatum maximowiczii*
Acer pensylvanicum
Acer platanoides Crimson King
** *Acer platanoides drummondii*
Acer pseudosieboldiana

Acer pseudoplatanus brilliantissimum
Acer pseudoplatanus leopoldii
Acer rubrum October Glory
* *Acer saccharinum lutescens*
Acer shirasawanum aureum
Acer sterculiaceum sterculiaceum
Acer tegmentosum
Acer tegmentosum White Tigress
* *Acer triflorum*
Acer truncatum Norwegian Sunset
Acradenia frankliniae
Aesculus hippocastanum
Aesculus indica Sydney Pearce
Aesculus mutabilis harbisonii
Aesculus × neglecta erythroblastos
Alangium platanifolium
Alnus glutinosa
Alnus glutinosa imperialis
Amelanchier grandiflora Ballerina
Amelanchier lamarckii
Aralia elata
Aralia elata aureovariegata
Arbutus andrachnoides
Aronia prunifolia
Azalea daviesii
Azalea Gibraltar (and others)
Azalea Holmbush
Azalea pontica
Azara microphylla variegata

Berberis valdiviana
Betula albosinensis septentrionalis
* *Betula ermanii* Grayswood Hill
Betula jacquemontii Grayswood Ghost
* *Betula × koehnei*
Betula Maurice Foster
Betula Mount Zao
Betula Mount Luoji
Betula papyrifera
Betula pendula
Betula Saint George
*** *Betula szechuanika*
Betula utilis Doorenbos
Betula utilis Forrests Blush
Betula utilis jacquemontii
Betula utilis Nepalese Orange
Betula utilis Wakehurst form
Buddleia alternifolia

Buddleia alternifolia argentea
Buddleia auriculata
Buddleia colvilei
Buddleia colvilei kewensis
Buddleia crispa
Buddleia davidii (several forms)
Buddleia delavayi
Buddleia fallowiana
Buddleia fallowiana alba
Buddleia farreri (*crispa* var. *farreri*)
Buddleia globosa
Buddleia japonica
Buddleia lindleyana
Buddleia Lochinch
Buddleia megalocephala
Buddleia nappei (= *araucana*)
Buddleia nivea
Buddleia nivea (pink form)
Buddleia nivea yunnanensis
Buddleia officinalis
Buddleia salviifolia (white form)
Buddleia wardii (*crispa* × *alternifolia*)
Buddleia × *weyeriana* Sungold

Callicarpa bodinieri var. *giraldii*
Callicarpa japonica leucocantha
Callistemon citrinus
Calycanthus floridus
Camellia japonica (numerous forms)
Camellia reticulata × *williamsii*
Camellia sassanqua (several forms)
Camellia transnokoensis
Carpenteria californica
Carpenteria californica Bodnant
Carpinus betulus
Carrierea calycina
Castanea sativa
Catalpa bignonoides aurea
Catalpa fargesii duclouxii
Ceanothus thyrsiflorus Millerton Point
Ceanothus (various forms)
Cedrus libani
Ceratostigma griffithii
Ceratostigma plumbaginoides
Ceratostigma willmottianum
Cercidiphyllum japonicum
Cercidiphyllum japonicum pendulum
Cercis canadensis Royal White
Cercis siliquastrum Bodnant
Cestrum parqui
Chaenomeles japonica
Chaenomeles speciosa nivalis (and others)
Chamaecyparis lawsoniana aureovariegata
Chamaecyparis lawsoniana nidiformis

Chamaecyparis nootkatensis pendula
Chamaecyparis pisifera filifera
Chamaecyparis pisifera filifera aurea
Chamaecyparis pisifera plumosa aurea
Chimonanthus praecox
Choisya ternata Sundance
Cistus (several)
Cladrastis lutea
Clerodendrum bungei
Clerodendrum trichocotum Carnival
Clerodendrum trichocotum
Cornus alba kesselringii
Cornus alba sibirica
Cornus alternifolia argentea
Cornus capitata
Cornus chinensis
Cornus contraversa variegata
Cornus Eddie's White Wonder
Cornus florida pringlei
Cornus kousa
Cornus kousa chinensis
Cornus kousa chinensis Claudia
Cornus kousa chinensis White Fountain
Cornus kousa Satomi
Cornus macrophylla
Cornus mas
Cornus Norman Hadden
Cornus nuttallii Goldspot
Cornus Ormond
Cornus sanguinea Midwinter Fire
Cornus Venus
Corokia × *virgata* Sunsplash
Corylus avellana
Cotinus coggyria
Cotinus coggyria Ancot
Cotinus Grace
Cotinus obovatus
Crataegus prunifolius
Cryptomeria japonica Sekkan-sugi
Cupressus macrocarpa
Cytisus albus
Cytisus battandieri

Daphne bholua Jacqueline Postill
Daphne × *burkwoodii* Somerset
Daphne odora alba
Daphne tangutica
Daphne × *transatlanctica* Eternal Fragrance
Daphniphyllum himalaense
Davidia involucrata
Decaisnea fargesii
Dendromecon california
Desfontainea spinosa
Deutzia calycosa Dali

Deutzia × *elegantissima* Rosealind
Deutzia hookeriana
Deutzia Iris Alford
Deutzia Mont Rose
Deutzia ningpoensis
Deutzia pulchra
Deutzia rosea plena
Deutzia scabra
Deutzia sechuenensis corymbiflora
Deutzia Strawberry Fields
Diervilla splendens
Dipelta floribunda
Dipelta ventricosa
Dipelta yunnanensis
Disanthus cercidifolius
Drimys lanceolata
Drimys winteri

Edgeworthia chrysantha grandiflora
Edgeworthia chrysantha Nanjing Gold
Eleagnus angustifolia Quicksilver
Eleagnus × *ebbingei* Gilt Edge
Emmenopterys henryi
Enkianthus campanulatus
Enkianthus campanulatus palibinii
Escallonia iveyi
Eucalytus pauciflora niphophila
Euchryphia glutinosa
Euchryphia lucida Pink Cloud
Eucryphia intermedia Rostrevor
Eucryphia nymansensis Nymansay
Euonymus alatus ciliodendatus
Euonymus alatus niphophila
Euonymus alatus Rudy Haag
Euonymus europaeus
Euonymus fortunei Interbolwi
Euonymus fortunei Silver Queen
Euonymus hamiltonianus Koi Boy
Euonymus hamiltonianus sieboldianus calocarpus
Euonymus japonicus latifolius albomarginatus
Euonymus maximowiczianus
Euonymus pauciflora niphophila
Euphorbia mellifera
Exochorda giraldii
Exochorda × *macrantha*
Exochorda serratifolia

Fabiana imbricata
Fagus sylvatica
Fagus sylvatica Dawyck
Fagus sylvatica heterophylla
Fagus sylvatica Mercedes
Fagus sylvatica purpurea
Fagus sylvatica purpurea pendula

Fatsia japonica
Fothergilla gardenii
Fraxinus excelsior
Fraxinus excelsior jaspidea
Fraxinus ornus
Fraxinus sieboldiana mariesii
Fremontodendron California Glory

Garrya eliptica
Ginkgo biloba
Gunnera manicata

Halesia monticola
Hamamelis × *intermedia* Jelena
Hamamelis × *intermedia* pallida
Heptacodium miconioides
Hippocrepis emerus (*Coronilla emurus*)
Hoheria sexstylosa, (and others)
Hydrangea arborescens Annabelle
Hydrangea aspera macrophylla
Hydrangea petiolaris
Hydrangea quercifolia (and several other forms)
Hypericum Winter Spirit

Idesia polycarpa
Ilex altaclerensis Golden King
Ilex aquifolium Silver Queen
Indigofera sp.

Juglans regia
Juniperus chinensis × *expansa aureospicata*
Juniperus horizontalis
Juniperus media pfitzeriana
* *Juniperus recurva coxii*
* *Juniperus rigida*

Kolkwitzia amabilis
Koelreuteria paniculata

*** *Larix kaempferi* Blue Haze
Larix × *marschlinsii*
Leiophyllum buxifolium
Leptospermum grandiflorum
Leptospermum scoparium Adrianne
Ligustrum vulgare variegatum
Liquidambar × *acalycina*
Liquidambar styraciflua
Liquidambar styraciflua aurea
*** *Liquidambar styraciflua* Lane Roberts
Liquidambar styraciflua variegata
* *Liriodendron tulipifera*
* *Liriodendron tulipifera aureomarginatum*
Lonicera elisae
Lonicera fragrantissima

Lonicera infundibuliformis rockii
Lonicera korolkowii zabelii
Lonicera ledebourii
Lonicera setifera daphnis
Luma apiculata (= Myrtus luma)

Maackia amurensis
Magnolia Atlas
Magnolia Black Tulip
Magnolia Caerhays Belle
Magnolia Charles Coates
Magnolia Daphne
Magnolia Joli Pompom
Magnolia kewensis Wada's Memory
Magnolia liliflora nigra
Magnolia × loebneri Leonard Merrill
Magnolia sapaensis
Magnolia × soulangeana
Magnolia × soulangeana Just Jean
Magnolia × soulangeana Star Wars
Magnolia stellata
Magnolia stellata Jane Platt
Magnolia stellata Royal Star
Magnolia stellata Water Lily
Magnolia tripetala
Magnolia virginiana Moonglow
Magnolia wieseneri
Magnolia wilsonii
Mahonia aquifolium
Mahonia aquifolium versicolor
Mahonia bealei
Mahonia lomariifolia
Mahonia Soft Caress
Mahonia × media Charity
Malus transitoria
* Malus tschonoskii
Metasequoia glyptostroboides Ogon
Michelia Fairy Blush
Morus alba pendula
Myrtus communis

Nandina domestica
Nandina domestica variegata
Neillia thibetica
Neoshirakia japonica
Nyssa aquatica
Nyssa leptophylla
Nyssa sinensis
Nyssa sylvatica
Nyssa sylvatica Autumn Cascade
Nyssa sylvatica Isobel Grace
Nyssa sylvatica Red Rage

Osmanthus × burkwoodii

Osmanthus decorus
Osmanthus delavayi
Osmanthus delavayi latifolius
Osmanthus yunnanensis

Parrotia persica
Parrotia subaequalis
Parrotiopsis jacquemontiana
* Paulownia kawakamii
* Paulownia tomentosa
Persicaria polymorpha (and others)
Philadelphus Belle Etoile
Philadelphus coronarius
Philadelphus coronarius aureus
Philadelphus delavayi melanocalyx
Philadelphus lemoinei
Philadelphus maculatus
Philadelphus Minnesota Snowflake
Philadelphus purpurascens
Philadelphus Virginal
Physocarpus opulifolius aurea
Physocarpus opulifolius Diable d'Or
* Picea brewerana
* Picea orientalis aurea
Picea pungens kosteriana
Picea smithiana
Picrasma quassioides
Pieris formosa
Pieris formosa forrestii
Pieris formosa forrestii Wakehurst
Pieris japonica (and several other forms)
Pileostegia viburnoides
* Pinus armandii
Pinus koraiensis
Pinus sylvestris
Pinus sylvestris fastigiata
Pinus wallichiana
Pittosporum heterophyllum
Pittosporum ralphii variegata
Poliothyrsis sinensis
Polylepis australis
Pontaderia cordata lancifolia
Populus × canadensis robusta
Populus lasiocarpa
Populus nigra
Populus wilsonii
Prunus avium
Prunus himalaica
Prunus incisa Kojo-no-mai
Prunus lusitanica variegata
Prunus Okame
Prunus padus colorata
Prunus padus waterii
Prunus Pink Shell

Prunus serrula Dorothy Clive
Prunus serrulata Ukon
Prunus Shirotae
Prunus subhirtella autumnalis
Prunus subhirtella Fukubana
Prunus Tai-Haku
* Prunus yedoensis pendula
Pseudolarix amabilis
Pterostyrax psylophyllus
Pyrus salicifolia pendula

* Quercus heterophylla
Quercus ilex
Quercus macranthera
Quercus palustris
Quercus phillyrioides
Quercus pontica
Quercus robur
Quercus rubra
Quercus velutina rubrifolia

Rhamnus alaternus argenteovariegata
Rhaphiolepis umbellata
Rhododendron azalea (several forms)
Rhododendron catawbriense grandiflora
Rhododendron cilipense
Rhododendron Hotei
Rhus potaninii
Robinia pseudoacacia
Robinia pseudacacia frisia
Rubus cockburnianus Golden Vale
Rubus thibetanus

Sambucus nigra Black Lace
Sambucus nigra canadensis maxima
Sambucus nigra laciniata
Sarcococca confusa
Sarcococca ruscifolia
Sequoia sempervirens
Sequoiadendron giganteum Wellingtonia
Sinocalycanthus chinensis (Calycanthus chinensis)
Sorbus bulleyana
Sorbus caloneura
Sorbus cashmeriana
Sorbus commixta Embley
Sorbus hemsleyi
Sorbus hupehensis
* Sorbus mitchellii (Sorbus thibetica John Mitchell)
Sorbus sargentiana
Sorbus vilmorinii Pink Charm
Sorbus Wisley Gold
Staphylea colchica
Staphylea holocarpa rosea
Staphylea pinnata

Stewartia pseudocamellia
Styrax hemsleyanus
Styrax japonica
Syringa sweginzowii
Syringa × persica
Syringa vulgaris Katherine Havemeyer
Syringa vulgaris Mme Lemoine (and others)

Taxodium ascendens
Taxodium distichum
Taxus baccata
Taxus baccata fastigiata
Teucrium fruticans
Tilia cordata
Tilia cordata Winter Orange
Tilia dasystyla caucasica
Tilia henryana
Tilia maximowicziana
* Tilia mongolica
Tilia platyphyllos

Ulmus × hollandica aurea
Ulmus minor vulgaris

Viburnum × bodnantense Charles Lamont
Viburnum × burkwoodii Anne Russell
Viburnum × carlcephalum
Viburnum fragrans
Viburnum henryi
Viburnum juddii
Viburnum plicatum Lanarth
Viburnum rhytidophyllum
Viburnum sargentii Onondaga
Viburnum tinus
Vitex agnus castus Silver Spire

Weigela florida variegata
Weigela looymansii aurea

Xanthoceras sorbifolium
Xanthorhiza simplissima

Zabelia triflora
Zanthoxylum piperitum
Zenobia pulverulenta

Roses at Daws Hall

Guinée, 1938
Rambling Rector, Multiflora, *c.*1820

Cecile Brunner (up chestnut), China, 1880
Golden Showers (on garage), 1956
Paul's Himalayan Musk (up chestnut), Moschata, 1822
Pompon de Paris, Chinensis, 1839
Old Pink Moss, Moss, pre-1700
Phyllis Bide (back of woodshed), Rambler, 1923
R. foliolosa, 1880
La Noblesse, Centifolia, 1857
Sombreuil (up magnolia), Climbing Tea, 1850

Alain Blanchard, Gallica, 1839
Golden Wings, 1956
Fantin Latour, Centifolia, *c.*1840
Général Kléber, Moss, 1856
Mme Plantier, Alba, 1935
R. moyesii Geranium, 1890
R. virginiana, 1909
Rosa Mundi, Gallica, *c.*1150
Rose de Rescht, Portland, 1850
Variegata di Bologna, Bourbon, 1909
William Lobb, Moss, 1855

Agatha, Gallica, 1810
Alba Maxima, Alba, *c.*1580
Alberic Barbier, Wichuriana, 1900
Albertine, Wichuriana, 1921
Alfred de Dalmar, Moss, 1855
Aloha, 1949
Baron Girod de l'Ain, 1897
Bellard, old
Belle Isis, Gallica, 1845
Blanc de Vibert, 1847
Blanc Double de Coubert, Rugosa, 1892
Blairii No.2, Bourbon, 1845
Blanche Moreau, Moss, 1880
Bleu Magenta, Multiflora, 1900
Blush Noisette, Noisette, *c.*1780
Boule de Neige, Bourbon, 1867
Buff Beauty, Gallica, 1939

Camaieux, Gallica, 1830
Capitaine John Ingram, Moss, 1856
Celestial (Céleste), Alba, *c.*1490
Chapeau de Napoléon, Centifolia, 1826
Charles de Mills, Gallica, *c.*1800
Claire Austin, modern
Commandant Beaurepaire, Bourbon, 1874
Complicata, Gallica, old
Comte de Chambord, Portland, 1863
Cornelia, 1925
Coupe d'Hébé, Bourbon, 1840
Crown Princess Margareta, modern
Cuisse de Nymphe, Alba, *c.*1470
Danae, Hybrid Musk, 1913
De la Maître d'Ecole, Gallica, 1840
Dembrowski, 1849
Desdemona, modern
Duc de Guiche, Gallica, 1821
Duchesse d'Angoulème, Gallica, 1835
Duchesse de Montebello, Gallica, 1835
Eglantyne, modern
Etoile d'Hollande, Hybrid Tea, 1919
Falstaff, modern
Fantin Latour, Centifolia, *c.*1820
Felicia, Hybrid Musk, 1928
Félicité et Perpetué, Sempervirens, 1827
Félicité Parmentier, Alba, 1830
Ferdinand Pichard, Hybrid Perpetual, 1921
Fraulein Octavia Hesse, 1909
Fritz Nobis, 1940
Général Kléber, Moss, 1856
Georges Vibert, Gallica, 1853
Ghislaine de Féligonde, Multiflora, 1916
Gloire des Mousseaux, Moss, 1852
Graham Thomas, modern
F. J. Grootendorst, Rugosa, 1915
Gruss an Aachen, China, 1909
Gruss an Teplitz, China, 1897
Honorine de Brabant, Bourbon, very old
Ipsilante, Gallica, 1821
Ispahan, Damask, *c.*1820
Jacques Cartier, Portland, 1868
Köningen von Danemark, Alba, 1826
La Belle Sultane, Gallica, pre-1700
Lady Penzance, Damask, 1894
Leda, Damask, *c.*1890
Lord Penzance, Sweet Briar, 1890

Lykkefund, Rambler, 1930
Madame Knorr, 1855
Madame Louis Lévèque, Moss, 1898
Madame Plantier, Alba, 1835
Manning's Blush, Sweet Briar, 1800
Mary Queen of Scots, Pimpinellifolia, old
Mme Alfred Carrière, Noisette, 1879
Mme. Hardy, Damask, 1832
Mme Lauriol de Barny, Bourbon, 1868
Mme. Legras de St. Germain, Alba, c.1820
Mme. Sancy de Parabère, Boursault, 1874
Mrs Anthony Waterer, Rugosa, 1898
Natalie Nypels, Floribunda, 1919
Old Blush, China, 1789
Old Pink Moss, Moss, pre-1700
Old Yellow Scotch, Pimpinellifolia, c.1850
Paul's Early Blush, Hybrid Perpetual, 1893
Paul's Himalayan Musk, Moschata, c.1890
Paul's Yellow Pillar, 1915
Penelope, Hybrid Musk, 1924
Perle des Jardins, Tea, 1874
Phyllis Bide, Rambler, 1923
Pomifera Duplex (Wolley-Dod's Rose), 1900
Pompon de Paris, Chinensis, 1839
President de Seze, Gallica, 1828
Princess Louise, Sempervirens, 1829
Prolifera de Redouté, Centifolia, 1820
Quatre Saisons Blanc Mousseaux, Moss, c.1800
Rambling Rosie, modern
R. banksiae lutea, 1870
R. centifolia Muscosa, Moss, c.1650
R. dupontii, c.1805
R. ecae, 1840
R. elegantula persetosa, 1914
R. fedshenkoana, 1880
R. foetida, pre-1590
R. foetida bicolor, pre-1590
R. gallica officinalis, Gallica, pre-1220
R. glauca carmenetta, 1923
R. glauca (rubrifolia), 1830
R. multiflora carnea, 1804
R. nutkana, 1876
R. pimpinellifolia Stanwell Perpetual, 1838
R. primula, 1910
R. roxburghii, 1814
R. rugosa typica, Rugosa, c.1780
R. sericea omeiensis pteracantha, 1890
Reine des Violettes, Hybrid Perpetual, 1860
Roger Lamberlin, Hybrid Perpetual, 1890
Rosa Mundi (R. gallica versicolor), Gallica, c.1150
Rose de Rescht, Portland, 1850
Sissinghurst Castle, Gallica, c.1850
Sombreuil, Climbing Tea, 1850
Soupert et Notting, Moss, 1874

Souvenir de la Malmaison, Bourbon, 1843
Souvenir de Mme Auguste Charles, Bourbon, 1866
Souvenir du Dr. Jamain, Hybrid Perpetual, 1865
The Crocus, modern
The Garland, Multiflora, 1835
The Pilgrim, modern
The Rambler, 1835
Tricolore de Flandre, Gallica, 1846
Tuscany Superb, Gallica, 1848
Veilchenblau, Multiflora, 1909
Village Maid, Centifolia, 1821
Ville de Bruxelles, Damask, old
William III, Pimpinellifolia, c.1820
William Lobb, Moss, 1830
York & Lancaster, Damask, pre-1550

VEGETABLE GARDEN
Adelaide d'Orléans, Sempervirens, 1826
Alchemist, 1956
Alister Stella Grey, Noisette, 1894
Frances E. Lester, Moschata, 1946
Laure Davoust, Rambler, 1834
Louis XIV, China, 1859
Princess of Nassau, Moschata, c.1820
Reve d'Or, Noisette, 1869
R. hemispherica, c.1600
R. hugonis, 1899
R. sancta, Gallica, very old
R. sericea pteracantha, 1890
Zéphirine Drouhin, Bourbon, 1868

Félicité Parmentier

Education at Daws Hall Nature Reserve

Daws Hall Nature Reserve is an ideal venue for a whole range of environmental education and outdoor leisure activities, for groups from pre-school to A-level and beyond.

Set in a beautiful 25 acre site with frontage onto the River Stour, there are a variety of habitats including woodland, wildflower meadows, grassland, ponds, and Losh-house Brook, a tributary of the Stour. There is also an observation beehive together with instructive wall charts. Our specialised equipment for moth and mammal trapping offers a closer look at creatures that are less often seen, before we release them back onto the reserve.

Our classroom is currently a small converted barn, for which groups have sole use during their visits. Classroom facilities offer the opportunity to introduce the site and topics for detailed studies, using microscopes and other apparatus, or to enter data collected for analysis. We have a composting 'eco-loo' at the furthest end of the reserve, so groups can stay out on the reserve for longer periods. Forest schools have an accessible activity shelter, fire pit and log circle, providing a fantastic base for toddler and family sessions. The Sanctuary Gardens with wildlife areas and a variety of wildfowl provide more opportunities to inspire and educate. Ninety percent of the reserve is accessible for wheelchairs.

The site is well equipped for environmental studies, ranging from sweep nets and bug boxes for invertebrate studies, to flow meters and chemical analysis equipment for soil and water sampling. All these provide a broad range of options for children of all ages.

Our Programmes

We offer schools a wide variety of programmes to comply with elements of the National Curriculum, GCSE and A-level Specifications, or simply to meet general interests and pleasure pursuits.

A day visit is usually from 9.30am to 3.00pm, but we are very flexible to suit the needs of each group. Due to limited facilities and the sensitive nature of the reserve site, we have a maximum group size of 50 for Primary groups in Spring/Summer, but highly recommend class-sized visits of 40 or less to get the best experience. For Secondary and A-level visits, we encourage a maximum group size of 30. We provide a personalised experience along with pre and post visit support. Please let us know of any special requirements when booking and we will do our best to accommodate you.

The following are examples of just some of the activities that can be offered to groups of all ages, at a very basic level for EYFS, or at increasing depth and complexity for different age groups through primary and secondary key stages, to A-level students and adults.

Examples of Activity Options

Minibeasts (terrestrial invertebrate studies): Search for invertebrates in different habitats. Students use collecting trays, bug boxes, sweep nets, beating trays, pooters and recording sheets. Identification sheets and keys are used to identify and classify finds. Comparisons can be made between woodland

and meadow habitats. How species have adapted to their environment and their roles within food chains and webs can also be considered.

Pond dipping (aquatic invertebrate studies): Use of pond nets to collect freshwater invertebrates from the dipping pond. Identification can be made using keys and producing scientific drawings of specimens, while discussing life cycles and water quality.

Kick-sampling in the brook: An activity enjoyed by all ages. Special nets are used to collect creatures that live in moving water, these are placed in sampling trays where their structure and movement can be examined, together their role as biological indicators of water quality.

River Work and the Water Cycle: The River Stour, Losh-house Brook, Pitmire Island and the flood plain all provide perfect resources to study river processes, water flow and the water cycle. The brook is small enough to stand in wearing wellingtons to collect measurements and record flow speed. Pollution studies and water quality can also link with biological sampling.

Map Skills: Field geography skills can be practised using our professional orienteering course, examining coordinates and features on Daws Hall site maps, and using OS maps of the wider area.

Plant Studies: Practise plant identification in different habitats together with studying growth and distribution, reproduction, and seed dispersal. Use of transects to observe changes in plant communities and exploring the reasons for these changes. Examine numerous native wildflowers and trees, and create guides to take away.

Creative Activities: Using natural materials found on the reserve creating anything from a leaf crown to a stick pyramid, a willow mini-raft, or a child-sized den. Our site is also perfect to inspire art and photography at all levels, together with creative writing, outdoor music and drama. We can also include mindfulness and environmental ethics within a session.

Seasonal Specialities: As we are open all year round, different opportunities present themselves according to the season. These vary from seeing thousands of snowdrops in February, flowers galore in spring and summer, amazing autumn colours in late October, and festive fun in the woodland in December. Geography visits can be made early in the year when landscape features are most visible.

Community Open Days: These give visitors the opportunity to see the garden, which has a wide variety of rare and unusual trees and shrubs, together with over a hundred different roses, all of which are labelled. Guided tours of the garden can be arranged for WI groups, garden societies and other organisations on request.

Contact Us

For more information about courses on the reserve or to see if we can meet your requirements please contact our Head of Education, Amy Sutcliffe, call on 01787 269766, or email info@dawshallnature.co.uk

For all garden group tour enquiries, please call: 01787 269213

Or visit our website: www.dawshallnature.co.uk